TU[illegible]DLE

TURDLE

Logic Puzzles to Solve While You're on the Loo

I.P. FREELY

bl!nk

First published in the UK by Blink Publishing
An imprint of Bonnier Books UK
5th Floor, HYLO, 105 Bunhill Row,
London, EC1Y 8LZ

A CIP catalogue record for this book is available from the British Library.

Paperback ISBN: 9781785122149

Also available as an ebook

3 5 7 9 10 8 6 4

Design and Typeset by Envy Design Ltd
Printed and bound in Great Britain by Clays Ltd, Elcograf S.p.A.

FSC www.fsc.org MIX Paper | Supporting responsible forestry FSC® C018072

The authorised representative in the EEA is
Bonnier Books UK (Ireland) Limited.
Registered office address: Floor 3, Block 3, Miesian Plaza,
Dublin 2, D02 Y754, Ireland
compliance@bonnierbooks.ie

www.bonnierbooks.co.uk

Dedicated to the silent but deadly

CONTENTS

No s**t,
Sherlock

SOLUTION AND ABLUTIONS: INTRODUCTION

'Sitting here all broken hearted
I meant to poop but only farted
The truth is stranger than a lie
Beware the clues lest you may die'

Reader, we have called you here because we need your powers of deduction. Our lead investigator, Detective Thomas Crapper, requires you to be on his team. We are on the trail of a devious criminal who is masterminding a crimewave around the city. One known only as Morifarty. The above note was left at the scene of a crime and you must help to solve the mystery.

But beware, our prey is as deadly as they are cunning. You will need to be at your sharpest to avoid a (toilet) brush with doom.

You'll need to keep your wits about you, as well as a freshly sharpened pencil.

To get you warmed up, let's work through the mystery of the first case that Detective Crapper ever investigated . . .

No s**t, Sherlock

EXAMPLE PUZZLE

THE CASE OF THE MISSING POTTY

It was his first day of nursery school and, being that sort of child, Detective Crapper (or Thomas C as he was known then) insisted on bringing his own potty to nursery. When it went missing, there were three clear suspects.

DANIEL BOOGER

A lover of eating modelling clay, he is clearly capable of anything.

120 Centimetres * Dummy User * Blue Top * Nappies

SAMANTHA JAMSALAD

A particularly aggressive hoarder of both sand and water. Might she want one more thing?

95 Centimetres *Not a Dummy User * Yellow Top * Nappies

ARCHIE LADLE

Possessor of a permanently runny nose and now, perhaps, a magnificent potty?

90 Centimetres * Dummy User * Green Top * Big Boy Pants

Crapper also knew that there were three locations in which the crime could have taken place and that they had used one 'weapon' in order to get the potty from where it had been safely stowed.

THE LUNCH HALL
INDOORS
Carpeted with fragments of long-dried houmous.

THE TOY CUPBOARD
INDOORS
Permanently coated in glitter and the debris of old toys.

THE PLAY GARDEN
OUTDOORS
Covered in blossom from the apple trees blooming above the climbing frame.

A SLINKY SPRING
Taken from the toybox and stretched until near breaking point.

A WOODEN BRICK
Heavy and cumbersome but movable, just.

A FAIRY WAND
Broken and bent, but still usable.

But that alone wasn't enough to nab the thief.
He knew the following facts were incontrovertibly true:

- Whoever was in the play garden did not have a dummy in their mouth.
- Whoever had the Slinky Spring had fallen out over it with the child who was in the lunch hall.
- The one with the fairy wand was wearing a blue top.
- Samantha Jamsalad had a splinter taken out that afternoon.
- The potty was taken by someone who left their footprints in edible crumbs.

So, he created a grid to set out what he knew:

	Daniel	Samantha	Archie	Hall	Cupboard	Garden
WEAPONS Spring						
Brick						
Wand						
LOCATIONS Hall						
Cupboard						
Garden						

At this stage, it was made from pasta glued to sugar paper but he would go on to perfect his method with pencil and paper (and joined-up writing).

Once he had set it all down, he began to fill in the grid.

His first clue was that **whoever was in the garden did not have a dummy.** He knew that the only one of the three to have left their dinky-boo-boo behind was Samantha Jamsalad.

Therefore, he knew that Samantha was in the garden and marked her off.

But he also knew that only one of them could be in each location. This meant Samantha couldn't have been in the cupboard or lunch hall. Using a simple process of logic, neither Archie nor Daniel could be in the garden. This meant that he could strike them from his enquiries too. *Every positive correlation in a category allows you to discount the other alternatives in each row and column*, he thought to himself in his child brain.

	Daniel	Samantha	Archie	Hall	Cupboard	Garden
WEAPONS Spring						
Brick						
Wand						
LOCATIONS Hall						
Cupboard						
Garden		✓				

		SUSPECTS			LOCATIONS	
	Daniel	Samantha	Archie	Hall	Cupboard	Garden
WEAPONS Spring						
Brick						
Wand						
LOCATIONS Hall		✗				
Cupboard		✗				
Garden	✗	✓	✗			

He moved onto the next clue:

Whoever had the slinky spring had fallen out over it with the child who was in the lunch hall.

At first, he couldn't work out what was useful about two people falling out over a Slinky Spring. How was that a clue? It was a facile toy, after all. Oh look, gravity is still happening! The joy! The wonder!

But then he realised. A person cannot fall out with themself. This meant that the Slinky couldn't be in the lunch hall.

As a result, he was able to mark that off too:

		SUSPECTS			LOCATIONS	
	Daniel	Samantha	Archie	Hall	Cupboard	Garden
WEAPONS Spring				✗		
Brick						
Wand						
LOCATIONS Hall		✗				
Cupboard		✗				
Garden	✗	✓	✗			

Time for clue three!

The one with the fairy wand was wearing a blue top.

He knew that the only one who'd been wearing a blue top was Daniel Booger. So, it was Daniel who'd been holding the wand. And now he knew a positive, he could eliminate the other row and column. If Daniel had the wand, then Samantha and Archie couldn't have it. And logically, that meant that Daniel couldn't have the brick or Slinky.

		SUSPECTS			LOCATIONS		
		Daniel	Samantha	Archie	Hall	Cupboard	Garden
WEAPONS	Spring	✗			✗		
	Brick	✗					
	Wand	✓	✗	✗			
LOCATIONS	Hall		✗				
	Cupboard		✗				
	Garden	✗	✓	✗			

After a brief break for some juice and an oaty biscuit, he cracked on with the next clue.

Samantha Jamsalad had to have a splinter taken out that day.

Well, the only thing that could have caused a splinter was something wooden. And the only weapon that could have done that was the wooden brick! This meant he could cross out the other rows and columns, as no one else could have had the wooden brick and she couldn't have had any of the other weapons. But more than that, if he now knew that Samantha had the wooden brick and Daniel had the wand, then by a process of elimination that meant that Archie had to have the Slinky Spring! Stopping only for a short nap, he hurriedly filled out the next sections:

		SUSPECTS			LOCATIONS		
		Daniel	Samantha	Archie	Hall	Cupboard	Garden
WEAPONS	Spring	✗	✗	✓	✗		
	Brick	✗	✓	✗			
	Wand	✓	✗	✗			
LOCATIONS	Hall	✗	✗	✗			
	Cupboard		✗				
	Garden	✗	✓	✗			

Now that he had solved four of the clues, he had enough information to fill in a whole other section of the grid.

If Archie had the Slinky Spring and the Slinky Spring couldn't be in the lunch hall, that meant that Archie couldn't be in the lunch hall. And that left only one location where Archie could be – the toy cupboard. And if Archie is in the toy cupboard, then that must be the location for the Slinky. So, he added a tick there too, which then meant he could put a cross in all the other rows and columns in that section. This meant Daniel was in the lunch hall. And if Daniel was in the lunch hall, then so was the wand.

		SUSPECTS			LOCATIONS		
		Daniel	Samantha	Archie	Hall	Cupboard	Garden
WEAPONS	Spring	✗	✗	✓	✗		
	Brick	✗	✓	✗	✗		
	Wand	✓	✗	✗	✓		
LOCATIONS	Hall	✓	✗	✗			
	Cupboard	✗	✗	✓			
	Garden	✗	✓	✗			

Since he knew that Daniel had the wand in the lunch hall, he knew the wand was in the lunch hall. And since he knew that Samantha had the Wooden Brick in the garden, he knew the wooden brick was in the garden. And since Archie had the Slinky spring in the cupboard, then he could fill in the final section of the logic grid.

This meant he was ready for the final clue.

The potty was taken by someone who left their footprints in edible crumbs.

Immediately, he could tell this was a different sort of clue. It was a statement about the crime, rather than the location of the crime or the weapon.

Edible crumbs. So that couldn't be the garden or toy cupboard. Surely, even his classmates wouldn't eat tree blossom or glitter? Which meant the theft must have

		SUSPECTS			LOCATIONS		
		Daniel	Samantha	Archie	Hall	Cupboard	Garden
WEAPONS	Spring	✗	✗	✓	✗	✓	✗
	Brick	✗	✓	✗	✗	✗	✓
	Wand	✓	✗	✗	✓	✗	✗
LOCATIONS	Hall	✓	✗	✗			
	Cupboard	✗	✗	✓			
	Garden	✗	✓	✗			

happened in the lunch hall, which meant it had to be Daniel, who had used the wand to hook his beautiful potty away.

Rushing at once to the teacher, he regaled them with his grand theory. After several meetings with his teachers and about three years of trips to see a nice lady who showed him pictures of animals and asked him how they made him feel, he finished school and became a detective.

But he never forgot his method of solving crimes (or his potty).

When a spate of lavatorial-inflected murders arose, he knew he was the man to solve them with help from a trusty reader. And that's where you come in.

Follow the mysteries and use your problem-solving skills to figure out the culprit. Can you solve them all?

Don't worry if you get stuck, there's a section of **EXTRA CLUES** to help you along. And if you get really stuck, you can flip to the **ANSWERS** (but that would obviously spoil the illusion that you are an investigating detective – you'd be like one of those people who watches magic shows just to try and spoil the tricks. Look, it's your book, you can do what you want with it. Just know that if you do flip ahead, I think you should probably take a long hard look at yourself. That's all.)

Good luck. May the flush be with you.

SECURITY CLEARANCE: GAME ON THRONES

1 – THIS PLACE IS DEAD, SHALL WE GO SOMEWHERE ELSE?

Detective Crapper is called to a bar with a building site theme. Drinks poured into tiny traffic cones, chips served on shovels, you know the kind of place. The bar owner had gone to use the toilet and was never seen alive again. Can you work out what happened?

SUSPECTS

BENJI STONE

A graphic designer/drum'n'bass DJ, he has played sets at all the local bars apart from this one.

5'8" (but 6" on dating apps) * Left-handed * Dark brown eyes * Dark brown hair

DAN DANIELS

A juice entrepreneur/lifestyle coach, he is looking to expand his range of ginseng shots into local bars.

5'5" * Blue eyes * Right-handed * Bald but it's a choice

MR BOOM

A model and influencer, Mr Boom had been keen to arrange some free food and drinks in exchange for some content.

6'1" * Green eyes * Ambidextrous, 'like, genuinely' * Blond hair

LOCATIONS

THE SANDPIT

One of the rooms is a big sandpit with a whole yellow digger in it.

THE SITE OFFICE

A remote private part of the bar, where people can go to chill out and get away from noise and activity.

THE PORTALOOS

The toilets are themed like building site Portaloos. Barely enough elbow room to wipe.

WEAPONS

A SELFIE STICK
LIGHTWEIGHT
Made from sustainably sourced bamboo but certainly strong enough to bludgeon someone.

A BOTTLE OF COFFEE LIQUEUR
MEDIUM-WEIGHT
Used to make espresso martinis but available by the bottle. Hugely strong and pungent.

A KETTLE BELL
HEAVYWEIGHT
Left over from the early noughties-soundtracked kettlebell classes the bar has during the day.

CLUES & EVIDENCE

- The smell of coffee was overpowering in such a small space.
- The online influencer didn't want anything to do with the person who bought the liqueur.
- The selfie stick was 100% not in the sandpit.
- The selfie stick belonged to someone with no hair.
- **They found sand all over the body**.

		SUSPECTS			LOCATIONS		
		Benji	Dan	Mr Boom	Sandpit	Site office	Portaloos
WEAPONS	Stick						
	Liqueur						
	Kettle bell						
LOCATIONS	Sandpit						
	Site office						
	Portaloos						

WHO?

WHAT?

WHERE?

2 – CLEAN-UP IN AISLE 4

On his way home, Detective Crapper realises he needs to buy toilet paper. As he steps through the doors he is greeted by a police constable he knows. 'Detective,' the police constable says, 'thank goodness you're here!' A fellow shopper has been checked out, but who has done it?

SUSPECTS

HARISSA JONES

An accountant who lives locally. She had been shopping for fruit and vegetables (biscuits and gin).
5'2" * Right-handed * Blue eyes * Brown hair

LUCIAN GADD

An art teacher with incredibly firm opinions on aesthetics.
5'6" * Left-handed * Brown eyes * Bald

HUMBERT WILDE

A journalist with a lucrative Substack who appears on the radio regularly to decry modern snowflake culture.
5'10" * Right-handed * Grey eyes * White hair

LOCATIONS

BY THE BINS
Outside the supermarket there are huge lockable bins full of waste.

THE FREEZER ROOM
Where any frozen goods are stored when not on display.

SELF-SERVICE TILLS
Where you pack your own shopping, for free instead of them having to pay someone to do it. What a lark!

WEAPONS

A TIN OF SOUP
HEAVYWEIGHT
Ham hock and garden pea, in case you're interested.

A BOTTLE OF OLIVE OIL
MEDIUM-WEIGHT
Extra virgin but not first press. Fine for cooking but probably not a salad dressing.

A POISONED SLICE OF CHEESECAKE
LIGHTWEIGHT
Sicilian lemon, including light cream cheese and arsenic.

CLUES & EVIDENCE

- Humbert Wilde vomits at the first scent of the bins.
- Lucian Gadd once gave a life-drawing course to the person who poisoned the cake.
- Strangely, the tin of soup was half frozen.
- The person who was at the self-service tills had access to poison.
- **The murder was committed using a key ingredient in pesto.**

		SUSPECTS			LOCATIONS		
		Harissa	Lucian	Humbert	Bins	Freezer	Tills
WEAPONS	Soup						
	Oil						
	Cake						
LOCATIONS	Bins						
	Freezer						
	Tills						

WHO?

WHAT?

WHERE?

3 – LASTONBURY FESTIVAL

The next morning, Detective Crapper is called to the last day of a local music festival, where a festival attendee has been murdered. But who caused them to dance their last dance?

SUSPECTS

BOBO THE MAGNIFICENT

The leader of the children's circus workshops running daily during the festival. After all, what could be less creepy than a clown?

6'2" * Right-handed * Blue eyes * Blonde hair

JACKSON QUINT

An ageing rockstar who played the 1 pm slot on the first day and was found wandering around in a field 36 hours later.

5'10" * Right-handed * Brown eyes * Brown hair

CARINNA VERDIGRIS

Part-time musician and the owner of a vegan street-food van, renowned for her southern-fried jackfruit.

5'7" * Left-handed * Blue eyes * Brown hair

LOCATIONS

BACKSTAGE

A busy area full of packing crates of all sizes and shapes.

THE VIP TENT

A luxurious marquee complete with a mini bar and several flavours of kettle chip-style crisps.

THE FESTIVAL TOILETS

Dante himself could not imagine anything more hellish.

WEAPONS

A GUITAR LEAD
LIGHTWEIGHT
Heavy and strong. Deadly.

A PIECE OF SCAFFOLDING
MEDIUM-WEIGHT
Used to build the stage but wrenched free and capable of doing serious damage.

A BOTTLE OF EXTREMELY OVERPRICED BEER
MEDIUM-WEIGHT
Detective Crapper wouldn't waste beer that expensive – but people are strange.

CLUES & EVIDENCE

- Bobo the Magnificent was a big fan of the person who'd brought the guitar lead.
- Jackson Quint was found to have the scaffolding pipe stuffed into the back of his leather trousers.
- The bottle of beer was not found in the VIP tent.
- When they found her, Carinna Verdigris was weeping and crying 'Oh, the humanity.'
- **The body was found in a packing case for a drum kit.**

		SUSPECTS			LOCATIONS		
		Bobo	Jackson	Carinna	Backstage	VIP	Toilets
WEAPONS	Lead						
	Scaffolding						
	Beer						
LOCATIONS	Backstage						
	VIP						
	Toilets						

WHO?

WHAT?

WHERE?

4 – FLUSH GORDON

Another day, another rich man murdered. This one is a local businessman called Gordon Jones. 'Why have I been assigned this case?' asked Detective Crapper, 'is there a link to our mastermind?' The constable scratched his head. 'We believe he owns several toilets, guv.'

SUSPECTS

MILLICENT JONES

Gordon's wife and the prime beneficiary of his enormous life-insurance policy.

5'6" * Left-handed * Blue eyes * Blonde hair.

GERRARD VAN DE BORRE

Gordon's long-time business partner, who now stands to inherit the whole company.

5'4" * Right-handed * Brown eyes* Blond hair

CHAD CHADSON

Millicent's tennis coach. Detective Crapper is uncomfortable with how white his teeth are.

6'2" * Right-handed * Blue eyes * Blond hair * less than 2 per cent body fat * Benches just under 300 lbs

LOCATIONS

THE UNDERGROUND CINEMA

They have a private cinema built in a basement, including film memorabilia.

THE KITCHEN

A huge, gleaming professional kitchen. Detective Crapper isn't sure if it's ever been used.

THE HOME GYM

A gym the size of an average family home. 'But were they happy,' muses Detective Crapper.

WEAPONS

A BOWLING BALL
HEAVYWEIGHT
Of course they have a bowling alley.

A SMARTPHONE.
MEDIUM-WEIGHT
Huge and lined with platinum. You could take down a rhino with it.

A JAPANESE KITCHEN KNIFE
LIGHTWEIGHT
Fiendishly sharp and oddly beautiful.

CLUES & EVIDENCE

- Either Chad is the owner of the knife or it was found in the kitchen.
- Gerrard was terrified of the person the knife belonged to.
- The bowling ball was not found in the gym.
- The smartphone's lock screen is a quote saying, 'Those who don't lift are oxygen thieves.'
- **Blood was found all over a Chewbacca's head in the cinema.**

		SUSPECTS			LOCATIONS		
		Millicent	Gerrard	Chad	Cinema	Kitchen	Gym
WEAPONS	Bowling ball						
	Phone						
	Knife						
LOCATIONS	Cinema						
	Kitchen						
	Gym						

WHO?

WHAT?

WHERE?

5 – DEAD CALM

'You know, the toilet on a ship is called 'the head' because in the days of the original square-rigged sailing ships, sailors would go to the head of the ship, so the wind wouldn't blow it back over them?'

'Fascinating,' nodded Detective Crapper. 'Now if you could just show me where the captain's body is.'

SUSPECTS

CHIEF ENGINEER MASTERSON

One of the most senior officers aboard the cruise ship. Possesses the hungry eyes of an ambitious man.

6'3" * Hazel eyes * Black hair

HEAD CHEF JULIAN BRANDYWINE

An intense man who talks about 'no-one on this rust bucket appreciating my genius'.

5'6" * Green eyes * Blond hair

HARRIET OMBUDSMAN

A guest on the cruise. When she smiles, Detective Crapper shivers.

5'7" * Black eyes * Black hair * Too many teeth

LOCATIONS

THE SHIP'S SAUNA
INSIDE
You can hardly see a yard in front of you, it's so full of steam.

THE ALL-WEATHER VIEWING DECK
INSIDE
Sheltered from the elements, surrounded by glass.

THE SUNDECK
OUTSIDE
At the top of the ship. A long way down.

WEAPONS

A HYPODERMIC NEEDLE
LIGHTWEIGHT
Presumably stolen from the medical bay.

A TITANIUM BRIEFCASE
HEAVYWEIGHT
Virtually indestructible and deadly if delivered with enough force.

FAKE TREE BRANCH
MEDIUM-WEIGHT
Used when they have weddings on board, it comes complete with fake white blossom.

CLUES & EVIDENCE

- A lot of warm, damp white pieces of plastic were found.
- Chef Brandywine had a vendetta against the person who brought the titanium briefcase.
- The all-weather viewing deck has a low doorway that the tallest suspect avoids at all cost.
- Several witnesses saw Harriet Ombudsman outside.
- **Tests revealed that the captain died of lots of tiny puncture wounds.**

		SUSPECTS			LOCATIONS		
		Masterson	Brandywine	Ombudsman	Sauna	Viewing deck	Sundeck
WEAPONS	Needle						
	Briefcase						
	Branch						
LOCATIONS	Sauna						
	Viewing deck						
	Sundeck						

WHO?

WHAT?

WHERE?

6 – THE GRAVEYARD SHIFT

'And of course there was King George the second, who was reported to have died when he fell off the royal commode,' said the museum guide as the group tour walked past. *Who even knew that Flushingham had a Museum of Toilets*, Detective Crapper thought, before moving on to inspect the body of the murdered security guard.

SUSPECTS

PROFESSOR PORCELAIN
The most senior academic at the museum. He'll do anything to protect his specialism.
5'2" * Left-handed * Brown eyes * Brown hair

CYNTHIA BOONDOGGLE
She runs the giftshop and so, she believes, the whole museum.
5' * Right-handed * Blue eyes * Grey hair

BERNARD CUSTERMODE
One of the graduate students. He wants to revamp the museum and make it more interactive. (Not like that. That wouldn't be hygienic at all.)
5'11" * Left-handed * Brown eyes * Green hair

LOCATIONS

THE BACK GARDEN
OUTDOORS
A beautifully tended outdoor space complete with a Japanese zen garden.

THE MUSEUM LOBBY
INDOORS
A huge sign has the museum's motto up on the wall: 'Maxime sapientia est ex maxime latrina.'

THE STOREROOM
INDOORS
Back of the museum, there's the space for any exhibits they can't fit on display. The floor is carpeted in pieces of the quilted toilet paper they use to pack them in boxes.

WEAPONS

CHEMICAL VIAL
LIGHTWEIGHT
A vial of chemicals used to clean the exhibits. Deadly poisonous.

A STATUE OF A TOILET BRUSH
HEAVYWEIGHT
Detective Crapper couldn't imagine who wanted it, but still it existed.

A TOILET LID
HEAVYWEIGHT
Taken from one of the 18th-century Parisian exhibits. Solid marble.

CLUES & EVIDENCE

- Bernard Custermode used to be friends with the person the statue belonged to.
- Professor Porcelain had the vial of chemicals.
- The statue of the toilet brush was never in the storeroom.
- Either Bernard Custermode had toilet paper stuck to the bottom of his shoes or Professor Porcelain was in the back garden.
- **The body of the guard was found under a language that Julius Caesar would have understood.**

		SUSPECTS			LOCATIONS		
		Professor	Cynthia	Bernard	Garden	Lobby	Storeroom
WEAPONS	Chemical						
	Statue						
	Toilet lid						
LOCATIONS	Garden						
	Lobby						
	Storeroom						

WHO?

WHAT?

WHERE?

7 – A SYMPHONY OF DEATH

The second violinist for the Flushingham Symphony Orchestra has been found dead. Detective Crapper isn't actually sure how many violinists are in an orchestra but he deduces at least two.

SUSPECTS

MAESTRO CLIVE

The conductor and an obsessive perfectionist. No wrong note was to be tolerated.

5'4" * Left-handed * Brown eyes * White hair

HENRY HAMSON

A member of the orchestra who covets a seat as a violinist. Wound tight as a bow string.

5'11" * Right-handed * Blue eyes * Brown hair

MARGOT FITZHALLIGAN

The FSO's biggest fan. There's nothing she wouldn't do to help. Nothing. No thing. No thing at all.

5'8" * Right-handed * Green eyes * Strawberry blonde, make sure you write exactly that

LOCATIONS

THE CLOAKROOM
INDOORS
A musty cave that smells of mothballs and mints with hangers glinting in the gloom. It feels at any moment as if one might step out into Narnia.

THE BAR
INDOORS
Every available surface is covered in drinks poured for the interval. As far as Detective Crapper can deduce, a concert is something to listen to while the punters drink.

THE ORCHESTRA PIT
INDOORS
Where the magic happens. Seriously, when the orchestra aren't playing they have a magician.

WEAPONS

AN ETHICAL TOTE BAG
MEDIUM-WEIGHT
Sourced from sustainable hemp fields, its handles make an excellent garrot.

A TRIANGLE
MEDIUM-WEIGHT
Detective Crapper hadn't realised how heavy these actually were.

A SHARPENED VIOLIN BOW
Whittled to a point at one end, but by who and how, nobody knows.

CLUES & EVIDENCE

- The ethical tote bag was in the least surprising place for a bag to be.
- The strings of the bow were covered in red wine.
- A witness says the killer has eyes 'like lapis lazuli'.
- Maestro Clive has a pathological fear of hangers so cannot be near them.
- **Analysis of the wounds reveal they were made by something with angles that add up to 180 degrees.**

		SUSPECTS			LOCATIONS		
		Maestro	Henry	Margot	Cloakroom	Bar	Orchestra
WEAPONS	Bag						
	Triangle						
	Bow						
LOCATIONS	Cloakroom						
	Bar						
	Orchestra						

WHO?

WHAT?

WHERE?

8 – LAST ORDERS

'The last thing he said to me was, "I'm just off to unblock the gents, Mavis".' Mavis sobs. Detective Crapper pats her on the shoulder vaguely. 'There, there,' he says. Then, after a suitable gap, 'Did he manage to, by any chance?'

SUSPECTS

BIG DAVE

A hugely passionate and voluble patriot and stalwart of the Dog and Ballcock, he'd die for this pub. But would he kill?
6'1" * Right-handed * Brown eyes * Brown hair

LITTLE DAVE

The pub clown. Also believes the governments control us through mind-control chemicals released from planes.
5'6" * Right-handed * Blue eyes * White hair

DAVE DAVE

Neither noticeably tall nor short. He tried to get the nickname 'Double D' going for a while, but it didn't take.
5'8" * Left-handed * Blue eyes * Bald

LOCATIONS

THE PUBLIC BAR
INDOORS
Decorated with paraphernalia of toilet equipment through the ages, which hangs from the ceiling.

THE SNUG
INDOORS
The bench tables are covered in beermats with hilarious cartoons on them.

THE CELLAR
INDOORS
A dark, damp place full of pipes and barrels. And boxes of crisps.

WEAPONS

AN EMPTY BEER BARREL
HEAVYWEIGHT
Even empty it is heavy enough to crush a human skull. It still has the dregs of old beer in it.

A DART
LIGHTWEIGHT
Could do someone a right mischief if delivered with enough force.

A POISONED PORK SCRATCHING
LIGHTWEIGHT
The normal ones will kill you eventually. But this one will within minutes.

CLUES & EVIDENCE:

- Belying his heft, this Dave is delicate and will only drink somewhere he is sure his pint won't leave a stain on the table.
- This Dave is terrified of dark places because his small stature means he was zipped inside a suitcase on a school trip when he was a child.
- Dave Dave is a staunch vegetarian and called out his fellow barfly when he saw his packet of meat-based snacks.
- The dart's flight was personalised with both the pub's sign and a Union Jack.
- **The body had traces of stale beer on it.**

		SUSPECTS			LOCATIONS		
		Big D	Little D	Double D	Public	Snug	Cellar
WEAPONS	Barrel						
	Dart						
	Scratching						
LOCATIONS	Public						
	Snug						
	Cellar						

WHO?

WHAT?

WHERE?

9 – FLUSH THE CISTERN

'That's exactly the sort of crypto-fascist propaganda I'd expect from you, pig,' shouted the young woman with blue hair. 'You want to know what killed him? Capitalism killed him! It's killing us all! Big Toilet owns this whole town!' Detective Crapper scribbled a note and then made his way back through the crowd of protestors to the place where the body laid.

SUSPECTS

TJ

TJ, or Tarquin Jones, is an eco-anarcho-crypto-revolutionary. His parents are both successful commercial barristers and his older sister owns a line of organic baby snacks.

6'2" * Right-handed * Blue eyes * Green hair

POPPY BANNISTER

Has devoted her life to campaigning for causes she believes in. She would do anything for them.

5'6" * Left-handed * Green eyes * White hair

LITTLE DAVE

Little Dave originally thought this was a protest about ULEZ, or lizards in human form. But now he's here, there's still plenty to get riled up about.

5'6" * Right-handed * Blue eyes * White hair

LOCATIONS

THE STATUE
OUTDOORS
In honour of the founder of Flushingham, Sir Arthur Ubends-Wonky. He was a very odd man.

THE ROUNDABOUT
OUTDOORS
The only roundabout in Flushingham. Decorated with daffodils in the shape of a toilet roll.

THE FLUSH AND HOPE PUB
INDOORS
Winner of the real ale prize for the last decade. At any one time, the atmosphere is more than 50 per cent beard dust.

WEAPONS

A BORIS JOHNSON MASK
LIGHTWEIGHT
Wrapped around the victim's face, it could certainly asphyxiate someone.

A PLACARD
MEDIUM-WEIGHT
Detective Crapper notices two errors of spelling and one of grammar. The paint on it is still wet.

A BOTTLE OF WATER LACED WITH DRAIN CLEANER
No-one should have insides this shiny. The smell of bleach is unmistakable.

CLUES & EVIDENCE:

- There was a single daffodil petal stuck to the placard.
- Poppy Bannister had history with the person who brought the Boris Johnson mask.
- Little Dave refused to go into any pub other than his regular one. 'If you haven't got loyalty, you haven't got anything,' he would often opine.
- Tarquin was already dreading what his mother and father were going to say about his paint-covered hands.
- **The body smelled of chemicals.**

		SUSPECTS			LOCATIONS		
		TJ	Poppy	Little Dave	Statue	Roundabout	Pub
WEAPONS	Mask						
	Placard						
	Water						
LOCATIONS	Statue						
	Roundabout						
	Pub						

WHO?

WHAT?

WHERE?

10 – BIDET OF THE JACKAL

The mayor of Flushingham has been murdered. Detective Crapper is the closest detective and rushes into the conference hall. Everyone and everything is a suspect. 'No one comes in, no one goes out!' he shouts.

SUSPECTS

GORDON BADGER

Owner of Badger's Ballcocks, one of the biggest employers in the area. A local business titan who will stop at nothing until he is the largest supplier of floating toilet mechanisms.

5'8" * Right-handed * Brown eyes * Almost no hair

GUSTAV BUBLET

A member of serving staff. Either he has a fake moustache on or he has a real moustache in the style of a fake moustache (which would be weird but not necessarily a crime).

5'4" * Right-handed * Blue eyes * Blond hair * A real or fake moustache

MINA JONES

A firebrand politician and the mayor's fiercest critic. She is campaigning on an anti-Big Toilet platform.

5'6" * Left-handed * Brown eyes * Dark brown hair

LOCATIONS

THE LIFTS
INDOORS
In a corridor lined with paintings of the town's glorious forefathers.

THE STAGE
INDOORS
The spotlight is broken and shining far too brightly.

THE FIRE ESCAPE
OUTDOORS
Littered with cigarettes and paper cups full of coffee.

WEAPONS

A CORKSCREW
LIGHTWEIGHT
Optimised for piercing corks and humans.

A FROZEN LEG OF LAMB
HEAVYWEIGHT
Presumably taken from the kitchen freezers. Easily heavy enough to murder someone with.

DENTAL FLOSS
LIGHTWEIGHT
Minty fresh but a possible improvised garrotte.

CLUES & EVIDENCE:

- Oddly, the corkscrew is still hot to the touch.
- Gordon Badger hasn't gone near a lift since 1997, after an incident he won't talk about. Even the sound of a lift pinging causes him to foam at the mouth and pass out.
- Mina Jones is such a hard-line vegan, she made them rename the meeting room at work 'the gathering room'. There's no way she could ever bring herself to touch meat.
- Gustav stinks of cigarettes. He even has cigarette butts stuck to the soles of his shoes.
- **The mayor was strangled. And smells noticeably of peppermint.**

		SUSPECTS			LOCATIONS		
		Gordon	Gustav	Mina	Lift	Stage	Fire escape
WEAPONS	Corkscrew						
	Lamb						
	Floss						
LOCATIONS	Lift						
	Stage						
	Fire escape						

WHO? ____________

WHAT? ____________

WHERE? ____________

SECURITY CLEARANCE: THE COP WITH THE SPLATTERY POO

11 – LIFE'S A BEACH

Things settled down a bit after the shock of the mayor's murder. Detective Crapper wondered if the few dots he'd found were even connected. Or was he in too deep, seeing patterns where there were none? It was almost a relief to get out of town and investigate a death at the beach.

SUSPECTS

BERNARD COLLINS

A retiree and dedicated fisherman, his piles make him prone to terrible rages.

5'8" * Left-handed * Brown eyes * White hair

BODIE DOYLE

He lives for the surf. Likes saying things like tubular and gnarly. Possibly hit his head on a rock?

6' * Right-handed * Blue eyes * Blond hair

GWYNETH CHALFONT

A passionate wild swimmer who hasn't missed a morning's paddle in over a decade, whatever the weather. She has biceps like steel rods.

5'6" * Right-handed * Brown eyes * Grey hair

LOCATIONS

UNDER THE PIER
OUTDOORS
The currents carry all the seaweed here, where it lies like a giant slimy beard.

THE HEADLAND
OUTDOORS
Full of fragrant grasses and sea herbs.

THE BEACH HUTS
OUTDOORS
Littered with old fishhooks and disgusting rotting bait.

WEAPONS

A METAL-TIPPED SPADE
MEDIUM-WEIGHT
Perfect for digging sandcastles and caving in a human skull.

FISHING LINE
LIGHTWEIGHT
Strong enough to hang someone with.

A DRIED STARFISH
With five deadly points. Nature's shuriken.

CLUES & EVIDENCE:

- Either Bernard Collins is responsible for the spade or the starfish was found by the beach huts.
- When Detective Crapper arrives, Bodie is limping. He then proceeds to pick a fish hook out of the sole of this foot.
- The starfish was almost missed as it was covered in so much seaweed.
- Everyone apart from one suspect was shivering with the cold. That suspect said they were used to it. The non-shivering suspect couldn't understand why someone had brought a spade like that to the beach.
- **The body is covered in tufts of grass seeds and, oddly, quite fragrant.**

		SUSPECTS			LOCATIONS	
		Bernard	Bodie	Gwyneth	Pier	Headland	Beach huts
WEAPONS	Spade						
	Fishing line						
	Starfish						
LOCATIONS	Pier						
	Headland						
	Beach huts						

WHO?

WHAT?

WHERE?

12 – DEAD OLD

'Well of course, some of the very oldest toilets here are worth upwards of £50,000 to the right collector,' said the woman who let Detective Crapper in when he arrived at Flush Antiques. 'Come with me, poor Larry is just over here.'

SUSPECTS

PENELOPE BANDOLIER

The financial backer for the shop. Sharp as a dagger.
5'7" * Right-handed * Blue eyes * Light brown hair

SIMON SIMONSON

A part-time helper at the shop. He is huge with hands the size of dinner plates, but also seems very gentle.
6'5" * Right-handed * Brown eyes * Dark brown hair

GARY CHUGGING

The delivery driver for the shop. He seems nervous.
5'8" * Left-handed * Blue eyes * Grey hair

LOCATIONS

THE FRONT OF THE SHOP
OUTDOORS
The shutters are still down and someone has recently sprayed 'Flushingham FC' on them.

THE LOADING BAY
INDOORS
Full of fragments of cardboard box, sticky tape and materials used to pack the antiques.

THE STORE ROOM
INDOORS
Stretching far back into the shop, a dusty space full of unseen treasures.

WEAPONS

A FINE EXAMPLE OF A BRASS TOILET BRUSH
MEDIUM-WEIGHT
A beautiful art deco-style piece. Heavy enough to do the job.

A RECEIPT SPIKE
MEDIUM-WEIGHT
For impaling paperwork – and what else? Deadly.

A CROWBAR
HEAVYWEIGHT
For opening packing cases. Not for birds to drown their sorrows.

CLUES & EVIDENCE:

- The toilet brush was found outside.
- When he interviewed him, Detective Crapper noticed that Gary Chugging was covered in dust.
- Penelope Bandolier brought the toilet brush.
- The tallest suspect did not bring the crowbar.
- **A constable was bent down looking at the body. 'What do you reckon that is, guv, spray-paint?'**

		SUSPECTS			LOCATIONS		
		Penelope	Simon	Gary	Shopfront	Loading bay	Storeroom
WEAPONS	Toilet brush						
	Receipt spike						
	Crowbar						
LOCATIONS	Shopfront						
	Loading bay						
	Storeroom						

WHO?

WHAT?

WHERE?

13 – A RECIPE FOR MURDER

Detective Crapper was rushing back to the station when he realised it was lunchtime. He stopped at Flushingam Fried Chicken, only to discover that one of the customers was dead. As well as about a hundred or so chickens.

SUSPECTS

FINN GITSON

A local youth who had stopped for Flushingam Spesh on the way home.

5'6" * Right-handed * Brown eyes * Brown hair

ARI VORN

One of the workers at FFC. He'd finished his shift but hung around for a lift.

5'11" * Left-handed * Brown eyes * Dark brown hair

MELONY BAKER

No, it's deliberately spelled like that. Her mum just really liked melons.

5'8" * Right-handed * Blue eyes * Blonde hair

LOCATIONS

THE CAR PARK
OUTDOORS
Someone has smashed a car window and there's safety glass everywhere.

THE CHILLER
INDOORS
Wreathed in freezing mist, like some ghastly scene from a chicken's nightmare. Lots of coleslaw.

THE TOILET
INDOORS
Up a narrow set of stairs on a corridor lined with posters of long-defunct bands.

WEAPONS

AN OLD-FASHIONED BROOM
MEDIUM-WEIGHT
Heavy enough to brush someone off this mortal coil?

A BOTTLE OF KETCHUP
MEDIUM-WEIGHT
Industrial sized and surprisingly hefty.

A KITCHEN KNIFE
MEDIUM-WEIGHT
Not particularly sharp, but sharp enough.

CLUES & EVIDENCE:

- Finn Gitson had an ongoing vendetta against the person who brought the kitchen knife.
- The kitchen knife was found next to broken glass.
- Ari Vorn's teeth were chattering when Detective Crapper arrived. Was that just from nervousness?
- The ketchup was found inside on the ground floor.
- **The victim was killed by something made of wood.**

		SUSPECTS			LOCATIONS	
	Finn	Ari	Melony	Car park	Chiller	Toilet
WEAPONS: Broom						
Ketchup						
Knife						
LOCATIONS: Car park						
Chiller						
Toilet						

WHO?

WHAT?

WHERE?

14 – NOW HE SLEEPS WITH THE FISHES

'Actually'. said the police constable, 'I don't think he is asleep.' Looking at the victim, Detective Crapper was inclined to agree. This was going to be a day that nobody at Flushingham Aquarium was going to forget in a hurry.

SUSPECTS

PROFESSOR PISCES

An expert in fish and passionate defender of the world's oceans. She doesn't even wee in them.

5'5" * Left-handed * Green eyes * Grey hair

GIL FLAPPER

A local celebrity chef. Sometimes he just likes to look at the fish and imagine cooking them.

5'10" * Left-handed * Blue eyes * Blond hair

RANDALL FINCH

He's slowly trying to wean himself off his severe hydrophobia. You can see the vein in his temple throbbing.

5'1" * Right-handed * Brown eyes * Brown hair

LOCATIONS

THE PENGUIN POOL
OUTDOORS
Someone really needs to clean this bit. Plastered in fish guts.

THE CAFÉ
INDOORS
Carpeted with burger bun crumbs and old chip fragments.

THE GIFTSHOP
INDOORS
Here you can buy everything from an octopus plushy to a pencil sharpener in the shape of a flounder.

WEAPONS

A NARWHAL'S TUSK
HEAVYWEIGHT
The closest anyone will come to being murdered by unicorn.

A VERY SHARP PENCIL
LIGHTWEIGHT
There's probably a joke about lead poisoning, except it's not actually lead is it – it's graphite.

A FEEDING BUCKET
MEDIUM-WEIGHT
Swung by the handle it could easily generate enough force to kill.

- 'Don't sniff the Narwhal's tusk, guv, it absolutely stinks.'
- As well as hydrophobia, Randall Finch also suffers from a phobia of fried food.
- Professor Pisces had once gone for a date with the person who brought the pencil.
- Tests revealed the bucket was almost definitely held by someone right-handed.
- **The victim was found beneath a piece of driftwood with 'Live, Love, Laugh' picked out in seashells.**

		SUSPECTS			LOCATIONS		
		Pisces	Gill	Finch	Penguin pool	Café	Giftshop
WEAPONS	Tusk						
	Pencil						
	Bucket						
LOCATIONS	Penguin pool						
	Café						
	Giftshop						

WHO?

WHAT?

WHERE?

15 – DEAD FUN

Detective Crapper hadn't been to Flushingham World of Adventures since he was a kid. There are more dead bodies here now.

SUSPECTS

ANGELICA BANDOLIS

A teacher at the local private school, here on a school trip.

5'6" * Right-handed * Blue eyes * Blonde hair

REGINA HARKING

One of the theme park staff. It was her job to walk around dressed as a 'Poppy Plunger'.

5'8" * Right-handed * Green eyes * Dark brown hair

GREG WU

A roller-coaster obsessive, here to try the new 'Round the U-bend' ride.

5'5" * Left-handed * Brown eyes * Blond hair

LOCATIONS

THE SHOOTING GALLERY

OUTDOORS

Here, fun-seekers can fire blasts of high-pressure water at targets (and each other).

THE QUEUE FOR THE PORCELAINATOR

INDOORS

Europe's largest toilet-themed ride.

THE ARCADE

INDOORS

Sticky with spilt drinks and covered in winning tickets, several thousand of which can be exchanged for a terrifyingly large teddy.

WEAPONS

A FENCE POST
MEDIUM-WEIGHT
Brought from somewhere else in the theme park and hefty enough to do someone harm.

A BOTTLE OF PILLS
LIGHTWEIGHT
If given in high enough doses, able to cause a heart attack.

A METAL ROD
MEDIUM-WEIGHT
It looks like it was from some sort of device for ordering queues, heavy enough to kill but small enough to be carried on a suspect's person.

CLUES & EVIDENCE

- The metal rod was either brought by Greg Wu or was in the queue for the Porcelainator.
- Regina Harking was hiding from whoever did bring the metal rod.
- The bottle of pills could not have been in the arcade.
- Greg Wu was seen by a witness pulling a fence post up.
- **The body was found somewhere very damp.**

		SUSPECTS			LOCATIONS		
		Angelica	Regina	Greg	Gallery	Queue	Arcade
WEAPONS	Post						
	Pills						
	Rod						
LOCATIONS	Gallery						
	Queue						
	Arcade						

WHO?

WHAT?

WHERE?

16 – THE MOST BEAUTIFUL CORPSE IN THE CEMETERY

The sound of screaming greeted them when they arrived at the Flushingham Beauty and Wellness Centre. But they quickly ascertained that the screams were coming from the waxing room. Once they'd apologised profusely and backed out of the room, they went to find the body.

SUSPECTS

HANNAH PLIMPTON

A tanning technician. She is the colour of expensive tropical hardwood.

5'4" Right-handed * Blue eyes * Blonde hair

MARTIN PRUNES

A masseur with hands strong enough to crack walnuts.

5'6" * Left-handed * Green eyes * Blond hair

JEB FUNDAMENT

A crystal healer and aura cleanser'. Detective Crapper thinks his teeth are too white to be human teeth.

5'10" * Right-handed * Green eyes * Black hair

LOCATIONS

THE HOT STONES ROOM

INDOORS

Where, apparently they put hot stones on people. The room is full of hot stones.

THE CRYOTHERAPY ROOM

INDOORS

This is where they make them really cold. Honestly, if they could just make up their minds.

THE ISOLATION TANKS

INDOORS

Where people pay lots of money to be locked in small, dark tanks full of warm, salty water.

WEAPONS

A WEIGHT WRAPPED IN A TOWEL
HEAVYWEIGHT
A perfectly serviceable improvised weapon.

A BOTTLE OF HEALING SERUM
MEDIUM-WEIGHT
Comes in a heavy, pointy bottle.

NAIL SCISSORS
LIGHTWEIGHT
Sharpened to a razor's edge.

CLUES & EVIDENCE

- The nail scissors were almost uncomfortably warm to the touch.
- Martin Prunes was good friends with the person who brought the serum.
- Hannah Plimpton has spent so much time under a sunbed she can't actually be in cold environments. She could die.
- Jeb Fundament was definitely in the isolation tanks.
- **Forensics say there were fibres of towel fabric found on the body.**

		SUSPECTS			LOCATIONS		
		Hannah	Martin	Jeb	Hot stones	Cryotherapy	Isolation
WEAPONS	Weight						
	Serum						
	Scissors						
LOCATIONS	Hot stones						
	Cryotherapy						
	Isolation						

WHO?

WHAT?

WHERE?

17 – THE ART OF MURDER

'Drawing inspiration from Duchamp's 'Fountain', this piece is a profound meditation on the transitive nature of memory and feeling,' read Detective Crapper. It certainly was a lot of toilets. A shame someone had killed the artist who'd made it on the opening night.

SUSPECTS

TIMOTHY CHALET

The owner of the gallery. There were rumours it was struggling financially.

5'6" * Left-handed * Green eyes * Brown hair

HAL HARLOW

A fellow artist. The victim had reviewed his previous show poorly on his blog.

5'9" * Right-handed * Blue eyes * Black hair

BENJAMIN TIFFLE

The art critic for the local newspaper. He vigorously defends his position as tastemaker.

5'11" * Left-handed * Brown eyes * Brown hair *

LOCATIONS

THE BACK OFFICE
INDOORS
Who knew art required so many spreadsheets?

THE GALLERY SPACE
INDOORS
Still full of discarded canapés and glasses of flat champagne.

THE TOILETS
INDOORS
Detective Crapper was almost entirely sure this was an actual toilet and not more art.

WEAPONS

A PALETTE KNIFE
LIGHTWEIGHT
Designed for spreading paint but sharp enough to kill.

A FRAME
HEAVYWEIGHT
A heavy-duty frame. Could certainly do the job.

A CHAMPAGNE BOTTLE
MEDIUM-WEIGHT
Capable of giving you a serious headache.

CLUES & EVIDENCE

- Benjamin Tiffle used to go out with the sister of the person with the picture frame.
- Timothy Chalet had the palette knife.
- The frame has definitely never been in the toilets.
- Either Benjamin Tiffle was in the toilets or Timothy Chalet was in the back office.
- **The body was found next to a tiny square of pastry with something mushroomy on it.**

		SUSPECTS			LOCATIONS		
		Timothy	Hal	Benjamin	Office	Gallery	Toilets
WEAPONS	Knife						
	Frame						
	Bottle						
LOCATIONS	Office						
	Gallery						
	Toilets						

WHO?

WHAT?

WHERE?

18 – SMOKING KILLS

No sooner had they left than they were on to the next case. The nearby vape shop was surrounded by police tape when they arrived and a curious crowd had gathered. The air smelled of an unholy mix of commingled ice peach, sour cherry and salted caramel.

SUSPECTS

HECATE VAN DUCKER

A former cigar smoker, he was told to quit by his doctor, so took up vaping. Which is fine. In fact, vaping is cooler, if you think about it.

5'8" * Right-handed * Blue eyes * Bald

SHARLENE TWIGG

One of the staff members. She has the shakes, as she passively consumes as much nicotine as those dogs they used to make smoke cigarettes.

5'3" * Left-handed* Brown eyes * Brown hair

MIGUEL BOSSANOVA

The town's champion ballroom dancer for the last decade. His favourite flavour is lemon meringue.

5'10" * Right-handed * Brown eyes * Black hair (died)

LOCATIONS

A BACK ALLEY
Full of pizza boxes from the takeaway place next door.

THE STORE CUPBOARD
Imagine the final scene of *Indiana Jones*, but with containers of vape liquid.

THE COUNTER
All of human life is here. Apart from people who don't vape.

WEAPONS

AN XL REFILL PACK (RASPBERRY COULIS)
MEDIUM-WEIGHT
Certainly big enough to bludgeon someone.

A HALF BRICK
Small enough to carry, big enough to murder.

A BALLPOINT PEN
Mightier than the sword, etc.

CLUES & EVIDENCE

- Having once injured himself slipping, Miguel Bossanova will never go anywhere with pizza boxes on the floor.
- Sharlene Twigg went to school with the person who brought the pen.
- The XL refill pack was too large to be displayed, so was kept in the only logical place for it.
- The pen is stored in a little stand on the counter.
- **The body had fragments of brick found on it.**

		SUSPECTS			LOCATIONS		
		Hecate	Sharlene	Miguel	Alley	Cupboard	Counter
WEAPONS	Refill						
	Brick						
	Pen						
LOCATIONS	Alley						
	Cupboard						
	Counter						

WHO?

WHAT?

WHERE?

19 – WORM FOOD

There has been a murder at the garden centre. This might be the first time there were actual daisies for them to push up.

SUSPECTS

JACK LOAM

A senior figure in the local allotment community with very firm ideas on biodiversity.

5'8" * Left-handed * Blue eyes * Grey hair

HELGA OMLIT

A self-taught experimental botanist. She's just asking questions.

5'9" * Left-handed * Green eyes * Brown hair

LONNY DIMBLE

He'd just wandered in to use the toilet, really. Or had he?

5'8" * Right-handed * Brown eyes * Grey hair

LOCATIONS

THE MANURE CORNER
OUTDOORS
It literally makes Detective Crapper's eyes water.

THE SEED LIBRARY
INDOORS
Everything from hardy perennials to weak non-perennials. Every surface is carpeted with a light dusting of seeds.

THE COMPOSTING ECO TOILET
INDOORS
It shines with a miraculous light. Surrounded by a beautiful gravel garden.

WEAPONS

A RAKE
MEDIUM-WEIGHT
Perfect for gathering dead leaves or leaving someone for dead.

A PARASOL WEIGHT
HEAVYWEIGHT
Designed to stop your umbrella blowing away.

A BAMBOO GARDEN CANE
LIGHTWEIGHT
Strong enough to stab with.

CLUES & EVIDENCE

- Jack Loam once had an argument in a café with the person who brought the bamboo cane.
- The bamboo cane also smelled strongly of dung.
- Helga Omlit is covered in seeds.
- The parasol weight was used to prop open the door of the seed library.
- **Tests revealed that the victim had a series of small puncture wounds in a regular pattern.**

		SUSPECTS			LOCATIONS		
		Jack	Helga	Lonny	Manure	Seeds	Eco toilet
WEAPONS	Rake						
	Weight						
	Cane						
LOCATIONS	Manure						
	Seeds						
	Eco toilet						

WHO?

WHAT?

WHERE?

20 – CURL UP AND DIE

Detective Crapper hated getting his hair cut. But presumably not as much as the victim whose death they were there to investigate.

SUSPECTS

MARNIE OAKWELL

A senior colourist and specialist in modern perms.
5'5" Left-handed * Blue * Blonde hair

NICK AULAIT

'As Michelangelo was with a paintbrush, so is Nick with a pair of scissors,' says one of his online reviews.
5'9" Left-handed * Green eyes * Blonde hair

KRIS RIGG

His girlfriend said he should go for something a bit more adventurous. But he's really not sure.
5'11" * Right-handed * Brown eyes * Brown hair

LOCATIONS

THE PERM ZONE
INSIDE
The chemicals they use are incredibly strong.

THE HAIR-DRYING ZONE
INSIDE
Similar in climate to the Sahara.

THE WASH ZONE
INSIDE
Where your hair is washed and conditioned with seaweed-infused conditioner.

WEAPONS

A CERAMIC HAIR STRAIGHTENER
HEAVYWEIGHT
Deadly, hot or cold.

INDUSTRIAL STRENGTH HAIRSPRAY
MEDIUM-WEIGHT
Strong enough to kill.

CUT-THROAT RAZOR
LIGHTWEIGHT
Perfect for detailing and murder.

CLUES & EVIDENCE

- The cut-throat razor had a faint chemical odour.
- Nick Aulait has the same dentist as the person who brought the hair spray.
- Marnie Oakwell believes that a senior colourist should not have to dry hair. In fact, as a point of principle she refuses to even go near the driers.
- Kris Rigg still had traces of seaweed in his hair.
- **The victim died after being hit by something heavy and hot.**

		SUSPECTS			LOCATIONS		
		Marnie	Nick	Kris	Perm	Hair-drying zone	Wash
WEAPONS	Straightener						
	Hairspray						
	Razor						
LOCATIONS	Perm						
	Hair-drying zone						
	Wash						

WHO?

WHAT?

WHERE?

SECURITY CLEARANCE: HERCULE BOGROLL

21 – SOMETHING FISHY

The bodies were on ice. More than he could count. Detective Crapper gazed around him with a feeling of mounting dread. Would he solve this case? Or would he flounder? 'That's very funny, guv. But shall we go and find the body?'

SUSPECTS

ERIC BASS

The owner and chief monger. He had the eyes of a man who had seen a lot of fish guts.

5'8" * Left-handed * Brown eyes * Light brown hair

GORDON DRIBBLE

A weekend worker who had big dreams of becoming a monger.

5'9" * Right-handed * Green eyes * Light brown hair

HORTENSE BECHEMEL

A local restaurateur with very high standards for her fish.

5'7" * Left-handed * Blue eyes * Blonde hair

LOCATIONS

THE BACK OF THE SHOP
OUTDOORS
The floor is slick with melted ice and fish juice.

THE FRONT OF THE SHOP
OUTDOORS
A trestle table with herbs and lemons for sale.

THE COUNTER
INDOORS
The fish scales get everywhere.

WEAPONS

A KNIFE SHARPENER
MEDIUM-WEIGHT
A heavy metal bar for sharpening knives on.

A FILLETING KNIFE
MEDIUM-WEIGHT
Deadly in the right hands.

A HALIBUT
MEDIUM-WEIGHT
Certainly heavy enough to do some real harm if swung hard enough.

CLUES & EVIDENCE

- The knife sharpener is slick, evil-smelling and cool to the touch.
- When he interviewed her, Detective Crapper noticed that Hortense Bechemel had a fish scale stuck to her.
- Eric Bass brought the knife sharpener.
- The tallest suspect did not bring the halibut.
- **The body was soaked in fish juice.**

		SUSPECTS			LOCATIONS		
		Eric	Gordon	Hortense	Back	Front	Counter
WEAPONS	Knife sharpener						
	Knife						
	Halibut						
LOCATIONS	Back						
	Front						
	Counter						

WHO?

WHAT?

WHERE?

22 – BED, BREAKFAST... AND DEATH

Detective Crapper is called to a popular local B&B. Unfortunately, for one guest, murder was on the menu too.

SUSPECTS

KATY BEANS

Comes in to do the breakfasts. Is a firm believer that the customer is not always right.

5'3" * Right-handed * Brown eyes * Light brown hair

GEOFFREY CHAFFINCH

Has been living here for two months after a 'misunderstanding' with his wife.

5'8" * Left-handed * Blue eyes * Thinning hair

EDNA THIMBLE

A reviewer for the local tourism website. Famous for her acerbic putdowns.

5'6" * Right-handed * Blue eyes * Grey hair

LOCATIONS

THE BACK GARDEN

OUTDOORS

A sandpit filled with rainwater is overlooked by a climbing frame slowly falling to pieces.

THE DINING ROOM

INDOORS

Breakfast is served from 8 am to 8.15 am. Toast crumbs coat every surface.

THE BATHROOM

INDOORS

Water temperatures are scalding hot or freezing cold with nothing in between. Travel toothbrushes can be hired for a small surcharge.

WEAPONS

A TRAVEL IRON
MEDIUM-WEIGHT
Portable and deadly.

COAT HANGERS
LIGHTWEIGHT
The sort that are locked to the wardrobe but this one has been ripped free, creating a deadly but rough edge.

A BOTTLE OF SHERRY
HEAVYWEIGHT
Old, sweet and capable of killing.

CLUES & EVIDENCE:

- Edna Thimble is afraid of climbing frames because she once fell off one as a child.
- Geoffrey Chaffinch once offered his seat to the person who brought the sherry.
- The travel iron has toast crumbs stuck to it.
- Katy hid her sherry bottle behind a plunger.
- **The murder was committed using something with a rough metallic edge.**

		SUSPECTS			LOCATIONS		
		Katy	Geoffrey	Edna	Garden	Dining room	Bathroom
WEAPONS	Iron						
	Coat hanger						
	Sherry						
LOCATIONS	Garden						
	Dining room						
	Bathrrom						

WHO?

WHAT?

WHERE?

23 – A DECENT INNINGS

Detective Crapper is called to the cricket ground. Someone has faced their final ball. But who is responsible?

SUSPECTS

HARRY BALLS

A decent number three batsman and a perfectly serviceable medium pacer. Took home seven mill' last year.

BASHER BUMPKINS

Once hit a six. Has been called Basher ever since.

OLIVIA HEATHCLIFFE

Married to the umpire. He takes a special pill half an hour before she arrives and has a lovely time.

LOCATIONS

THE PAVILION
INDOORS
A tea urn and some dry sandwiches.

THE DUCK POND
OUTDOORS
A right-handed hook shot means you've lost your ball.

THE OUTFIELD
OUTDOORS
The field borders onto the most popular dog-walking route around. About 50 per cent dog faeces.

WEAPONS

A CRICKET STUMP
MEDIUM-WEIGHT
Sharpened to a point.

A CRICKET BALL IN A CRICKET SOCK
MEDIUM-WEIGHT
Aah, the thwack of cotton and leather on human bone.

A CRICKET BOX
LIGHTWEIGHT
If held over the face would function like deadly ether.

CLUES & EVIDENCE:

- Harry Balls went to prep school with the brother of the person who brought the cricket stump.
- The sock with the cricket ball in it had the initials BB embroidered on it.
- The cricket box was not by the duck pond.
- Olivia Heathcliffe's shoes were covered in dog poo.
- **The body was found inside.**

		SUSPECTS			LOCATIONS		
		Harry	Basher	Olivia	Pavilion	Pond	Outfield
WEAPONS	Stump						
	Ball						
	Box						
LOCATIONS	Pavilion						
	Pond						
	Outfield						

WHO? ____________

WHAT? ____________

WHERE? ____________

24 – AT THE SHARP END

What could be safer than knitting? A lot of things, it turns out. Detective Crapper has been called to the Flushingham community centre. Can he untangle things?

SUSPECTS

HEN CHICKENS

Has recently moved to the area and is looking to make friends. People often say of him, 'If your surname was chickens, would you marry a woman called Henrietta?'

5'7" * Left-handed * Green eyes * Red hair

IVY TOOTER

The founder of the knitting circle. Rules it with needles of iron.

5'5" * Right-handed * Brown eyes * Grey hair

BEN DARCY

So proud that he's a young man who is into knitting that he can't stop smiling.

5'11" * Right-handed * Blue eyes * Blond hair * Loves knitting – I know right!

LOCATIONS

THE LOST PROPERTY CUPBOARD
INDOORS
Several decades of lost items, including false teeth, a false leg and a stuffed dog.

THE KITCHEN
INDOORS
Every surface is stained beige with discarded teabags.

THE GARDEN
OUTDOORS
Full of half-deflated inflatable toys and children's cars with missing wheels.

WEAPONS

A WALKING STICK.
MEDIUM-WEIGHT
Made from yew and burnished to a dark lustre.

A CRUTCH
MEDIUM-WEIGHT
Designed to help people move but capable of stopping them move forever.

A SMALL TEA URN
Big enough to kill.

CLUES & EVIDENCE:

- Either Ben Darcy brought the tea urn or it was found in the kitchen.
- Ivy Tooter had never trusted the person who brought the urn.
- The crutch was not found outside.
- Ben Darcy's most used hashtag is #WalkingStickLife.
- **The body was found slumped over a box full of used dummies.**

		SUSPECTS			LOCATIONS		
		Hen	Ivy	Ben	Lost property	Kitchen	Garden
WEAPONS	Walking stick						
	Crutch						
	Tea urn						
LOCATIONS	Lost property						
	Kitchen						
	Garden						

WHO?

WHAT?

WHERE?

25 – FLUSH TO THE FUTURE

'Here at Plop-X, we are exploring what the future of toilets looks like. With machine learning, with AI, with nano-technology and...' Detective Crapper stepped aside to let the tour past. 'The body is this way, sir,' whispered the head of PR.

SUSPECTS

NELO SMUK

The founder of Plop-X, described on his own website as 'a toilet visionary'.

5'8" * Right-handed * Blue eyes * Black hair

CHIEF SCIENCE OFFICER JIM BRANSON

Rumoured to be the real brains of the operation, though the public don't know that.

5'2" * Brown eyes * Brown hair

GWEN CHIPS

A junior team member. In thrall to Smuk and his legend.

5'7" * Blue eyes * Blonde hair*

LOCATIONS

THE GARDEN
OUTDOORS
Lined with cherry blossoms.

THE STAFF CANTEEN
INDOORS
Detective Crapper thinks this may be nicer than most restaurants he's ever been to.

THE IDEAS ROOM
INDOORS
Full of bouncy balls to sit on and a table football table.

WEAPONS

A PAIR OF PLYERS
LIGHTWEIGHT
Sharpened at the tip for holding delicate things.

A LAPTOP CASE
MEDIUM-WEIGHT
Made from reclaimed materials but that doesn't make it any less deadly.

WIFI-ENABLED TOILET BRUSH
MEDIUM-WEIGHT
Part of the internet of things.

CLUES & EVIDENCE:

- The toilet brush was covered in blossom petals.
- Jim Branson had a recent difference of opinion with the person who brought the laptop case.
- Nelo Smuk does not believe in food. He ingests his nutrients as liquid only. He cannot physically be near people eating.
- Several witnesses saw Gwen Chips in the ideas room.
- **Tests revealed that the body had wounds from two separate blades close together.**

		SUSPECTS			LOCATIONS		
		Smuk	Branson	Chips	Garden	Canteen	Ideas room
WEAPONS	Plyers						
	Laptop case						
	Toilet brush						
LOCATIONS	Garden						
	Canteen						
	Ideas room						

WHO?

WHAT?

WHERE?

26 – HE BOUGHT THE FARM

'We use only organic fertilisers!' shouted their guide over the roar of the tractor engine. 'Yes, yes, I think I can smell that,' shouted back Detective Crapper, before gagging. 'How much further?'

SUSPECTS

JED THRUP

Has worked at the farm as long as anyone can remember. He is as strong as an old oak tree.

5'8" * Right-handed * Brown eyes * Grey hair

FELICITY MELP

Operates an organic kimchi business out of a converted outhouse, using the farm's cabbages.

5'5" * Right-handed * Blue eyes * Blonde hair

NATHANIEL WEST

The owner of the neighbouring farm. There are rumours of a border dispute.

5'11" * Left-handed * Brown eyes * White hair *

LOCATIONS

THE ORCHARD
OUTDOORS
Full of the heady aroma of rotting, fermenting apples.

THE DAIRY
INDOORS
Complete with a sign saying, 'Pull the Udder One.'

THE OLD BARN
INDOORS
Now used mainly to store old rusting farm equipment.

WEAPONS

HAY RAKE
MEDIUM-WEIGHT
Sturdy and potentially deadly.

A SLEDGEHAMMER
HEAVYWEIGHT
Used for hammering in fence poles. And possibly enemies?

AN ANTIQUE MILKING BUCKET
MEDIUM-WEIGHT
Metal with a very swingable handle.

CLUES & EVIDENCE:

- Nathaniel West had once bought a drink in the local pub for the person who'd brought the sledgehammer.
- Jed Thrup would never let his special hay rake out of his sight. Rumour was he slept with it.
- The sledgehammer had never been in the old barn.
- Either Nathaniel West pricked his finger on a rusty saw or Jed Thrup slipped on a rotting apple.
- **The body was found under an inappropriately unserious sign.**

		SUSPECTS			LOCATIONS		
		Jed	Felicity	Nathaniel	Orchard	Dairy	Barn
WEAPONS	Rake						
	Sledgehammer						
	Bucket						
LOCATIONS	Orchard						
	Dairy						
	Barn						

WHO? ______

WHAT? ______

WHERE? ______

27 – YOU'LL NEVER GET THAT OUT

Their next call took them to Flushingham Clothes Services, which proudly claimed: 'There's no stain too big for us.' Judging from the police tape outside, that claim might be sorely tested.

SUSPECTS

BILLY LINEN

The owner of several clothes services in the region. There are rumours he has connections to organised crime.

5'6" * Left-handed * Blue eyes * White hair

GLADYS BAINES

'If God had wanted us to wash our clothes at home, he wouldn't have created laundrettes, dear.'

5'2" * Right-handed * Brown eyes * Grey hair

VERNON GUBER

A local university student. He has waited until everything he owns is dirty, turned it inside out, worn it again, and is now getting it cleaned.

5'8" * Right-handed * Green eyes * Blond hair

LOCATIONS

THE LAUNDERETTE ZONE

INDOORS

A succession of enormous washing machines. Someone has dropped a container of washing powder over every surface.

THE DRY-CLEAN ZONE

INDOORS

A miraculous technology that uses a pungent array of chemicals but no water.

THE ZIP ZONE

INDOORS

Where zips get repaired. Logical if Detective Crapper thinks about it.

WEAPONS

A VIAL OF SOLVENT
LIGHTWEIGHT
Used in dry-cleaning. Potentially deadly if ingested.

SPARE ZIPS
LIGHTWEIGHT
Could serve as an improvised garotte.

A BIG POLE
HEAVYWEIGHT
Used to pull the dry cleaning along the rail. A long piece of heavy wood with a big spike on it.

CLUES & EVIDENCE:

- The spare zips had somehow got washing powder on them.
- The big pole has a faint chemical tang to it.
- A witness said the killer had hair the colour of a 'white wash someone has left a black sock in'.
- Billy Linen is ironically allergic to washing powder, so takes pains to avoid it.
- **Analysis showed odd marks around the victim's neck – a series of vertical scores in a long row, like a tiny train track.**

		SUSPECTS			LOCATIONS		
		Billy	Gladys	Vernon	Laundrette	Dry-clean	Zip zone
WEAPONS	Solvent						
	Zips						
	Pole						
LOCATIONS	Laundrette						
	Dry-clean						
	Zip zone						

WHO?

WHAT?

WHERE?

28 – A GRAVE SITUATION

In many ways, a murder at a funeral parlour was just cutting out the middleman. But it did cause an awful lot of extra paperwork.

SUSPECTS

ROBERT IAN PETERS

The patriarch of the family business. Has seen more corpses than you've had hot dinners.

5'9" * Right-handed * Grey eyes * White hair

ROBERT IAN PETERS JR

Set to inherit the family empire.

5'9" * Right-handed * Grey eyes * Grey hair

ROBERT IAN PETERS III

The youngest member of the family. Still learning the family business.

5'9" * Right-handed * Grey eyes * Blond hair

LOCATIONS

THE OFFICE

INDOORS

Where the discussions around materials, styles and prices are discussed. Boxes of tissues everywhere.

THE MORGUE

INDOORS

Detective Crapper is no stranger to it, or its familiar odour.

THE DISPLAY ROOM

INDOORS

A collection of the most popular coffins and swatches of different weights of velvet.

WEAPONS

A COFFIN HANDLE
HEAVYWEIGHT
Solid brass and carries a real heft.

A FLOWER CANE
LIGHTWEIGHT
Used for flower arrangements. Incredibly sharp.

A CRYSTAL DECANTER OF BRANDY
Sometimes people need a little something to revive them-selves. But certainly heavy enough to kill.

CLUES & EVIDENCE:

- The oldest Peters has the faint but unmistakable whiff of embalming fluid.
- The next oldest Peters has velvet fibres on his cuff.
- The youngest Peters doesn't agree with alcohol and told the person holding the brandy so when he saw them.
- The only one who has access to the cupboard with the flower cane is Grandpa Peters.
- **The body had traces of brass on it.**

		SUSPECTS			LOCATIONS		
		RIP	RIP JR	RIP III	Office	Morgue	Display
WEAPONS	Handle						
	Cane						
	Brandy						
LOCATIONS	Office						
	Morgue						
	Display						

WHO?

WHAT?

WHERE?

29 – NOT A MOURNING PERSON

Early the next morning, Detectic Crapper was summoned to a local café. No one expects to die over their fry up. Well, not immediately anyway.

SUSPECTS

CLIVE THIMBLE

The head (and only) chef at Flushingham Café. He was suspicious of vegetables that weren't red or grey.

5'11" * Right-handed * Brown eyes * Black hair

JOHN BOMBER

A local plasterer who had his breakfast every morning at the café. 'Five sugars please, mate.'

5'6" * Left-handed * Blue eyes * Grey hair

JEZ BUNDLE

On a trip to curate London's best fried breakfasts for his various social channels.

5'9" * Right-handed * Blue eyes * Brown hair

LOCATIONS

THE KITCHEN
INDOORS
An experiment in what happens if you don't clean a kitchen.

OUTSIDE TABLES
OUTDOORS
There are two wobbly metal tables outside, covered in spilt sugar and tea stains.

THE BACK ALLEY
OUTDOORS
The ground is littered with fragments from the nail parlour next door.

WEAPONS

A COFFE MUG
LIGHTWEIGHT
Big and heavy.

A VASE OF PLASTIC FLOWERS
MEDIUM-WEIGHT
Detective Crapper thinks they were to add ambience, not an ambulance, but on second thoughts....

A FORK
LIGHTWEIGHT
Does the job if you need it to.

CLUES & EVIDENCE:

- There are sugar granules on the base of the vase.
- John Bomber got a bit wound up by the person who brought the mug.
- Jez Bundle had a pathological fear of back alleys and fake nails.
- Clive Thimble brought the vase.
- **The body had a series of four small wounds in a row.**

		SUSPECTS			LOCATIONS		
		Clive	John	Jez	Kitchen	Outside tables	Back alley
WEAPONS	Mug						
	Vase						
	Fork						
LOCATIONS	Kitchen						
	Outside tables						
	Back alley						

WHO?

WHAT?

WHERE?

30 – CRYPT, OH

In the hectic world of digital currencies, some people were making a killing. But someone at the Flushingham Tech Zone had been murdered. The question was, who did it?

SUSPECTS

JUNIPER FINCH
The creator of multiple food companies.
5'8" * Left-handed * Blue eyes * Blonde hair

KURT WOBBLE
Really into NFTs right now.
5'6" * Left-handed * Green eyes * Brown hair

LUNAR
He has actually changed his name to that. Legally.
5'9" * Left-handed * Green eyes * Shaved head

LOCATIONS

THE CAFÉ
INDOORS
Where they drink their cold-brewed coffees.

HOT YOGA ROOM
INDOORS
Because legally hot yoga must be everywhere now.

THE VAPING ROOM
OUTDOORS
Sheltered from the rain. Littered with vape packaging.

WEAPONS

A METAL WATER CUP
MEDIUM-WEIGHT
Keeps the water cold *and* saves the planet.

A DIGITAL NOTEBOOK
MEDIUM-WEIGHT
Light enough to carry in your bag but heavy enough to murder.

NOVELTY DATA STICK HOLDER
LIGHTWEIGHT
The data stick is long gone. Shaped like a devil with horns pointy enough to do serious damage.

CLUES & EVIDENCE:

- The metal water cup has been somewhere hot and humid.
- Juniper Finch is massively allergic to coffee. Even touching spilled coffee or breathing in air with too much coffee in it causes an allergic reaction.
- Lunar is doing an analogue cleanse. He has made a vow to not use digital tools for the whole month.
- Kurt Wobble has a serious vaping habit.
- **The victim was killed with a series of double puncture wounds next to each other in a regular pattern.**

		SUSPECTS			LOCATIONS		
		Juniper	Kurt	Lunar	Café	Yoga	Vaping
WEAPONS	Cup						
	Notebook						
	Stick						
LOCATIONS	Café						
	Yoga						
	Vaping						

WHO? ____________

WHAT? ____________

WHERE? ____________

SECURITY CLEARANCE: TURDBLOCK HOLMES

31 – PARK DEATH!

All the people, so many people... all unaware that there had been a murder committed in their midst. Apart from one person, the one who'd done it. But who were they?

SUSPECTS

MAJOR HENRY BURGERS

A retired army man. Never afraid to tell someone off for trampling the flowerbeds.

5'8" * Left-handed * Blue eyes * White hair

HUGO DANGLE

In the park to practise his circus skills.

6' * Right-handed * Blue eyes * Blond hair

MIRIAM FRIMPLE

A professional dog walker.

5'6" * Right-handed * Brown eyes * Brown hair

LOCATIONS

THE ORNAMENTAL FOUNTAIN

OUTDOORS

People used to come and throw coins in. Presumably now they just do a bank transfer. Someone has put washing up liquid in it.

THE ROSE GARDEN

OUTDOORS

Full of the rich scent of roses.

THE GARDENER'S HUT

OUTDOORS

Surrounded by a liberal sprinkling of manure.

WEAPONS

A GARDEN TROWEL
MEDIUM-WEIGHT
Perfectly possible to kill someone with this.

A DIGGING FORK
MEDIUM-WEIGHT
Caked in mud and surprisingly sharp prongs.

A TREE BRANCH
Nothing fancy but does the job alright.

CLUES & EVIDENCE:

- Either Major Burgers brought the garden trowel, or the tree branch was by the gardener's hut.
- Hugo Dangle has stepped in manure.
- The tree branch has traces of some sort of soap on it.
- Miriam Frimple saw someone with the garden trowel as she was walking a particularly lazy poodle.
- **The body smells like roses.**

		SUSPECTS			LOCATIONS		
		Henry	Hugo	Miriam	Fountain	Garden	Hut
WEAPONS	Trowel						
	Fork						
	Branch						
LOCATIONS	Fountain						
	Garden						
	Hut						

WHO?

WHAT?

WHERE?

32 – CORPSING

Detective Crapper had heard of comedians dying on stage, but he didn't expect one of the denizens of the Flushingham Comedy club to take the expression so literally.

SUSPECTS

SUZE O'MALLEY

A neat line in surreal self-depreciating one-liners.
5'6" * Right-handed * Blue eyes * Light brown hair

MILTON BOARDWALK

He does satirical songs.
5'8" * Right-handed * Brown eyes * Dark brown hair

LEONARD PILCHARD

The comedy reviewer for the *Flushingham Gazette*.
A frustrated comedian.
5'10" * Left-handed * Brown eyes * Brown hair

LOCATIONS

THE STAGE
INDOORS
Covered in the nervous sweat of performers.

THE BAR
INDOORS
Covered in stale beer and flat cider.

THE BACK ROW
INDOORS
Where everyone puts their chewed chewing gum.

WEAPONS

A MICROPHONE STAND
MEDIUM-WEIGHT
Capable of delivering the final mic drop.

A BOTTLE OF CHEAP WINE
MEDIUM-WEIGHT
One blow from this will induce the ultimate hangover.

A SWORD
HEAVYWEIGHT
A leftover prop. Not sharp enough to stab but certainly heavy enough to bludgeon.

CLUES & EVIDENCE:

- The microphone stand has human sweat on it.
- Leonard Pilchard is picking irritably at some chewing gum stuck to his trousers.
- Suze O'Malley brought the microphone stand.
- The suspect with the ukulele did not bring the sword.
- **The victim died on stage, remember.**

		SUSPECTS			LOCATIONS		
		Suze	Milton	Leonard	Stage	Bar	Back row
WEAPONS	Mic stand						
	Wine						
	Sword						
LOCATIONS	Stage						
	Bar						
	Back row						

WHO

WHAT?

WHERE?

33 – CAKES TO DIE FOR

Detective Crapper didn't really get cupcakes. They were just a little cake. Surely you wanted a big cake. A proper-sized cake. He'd never understand. 'OK, guv. Shall we check out this body, then?'

SUSPECTS

CHARLOTTE MYNG

The owner of the cupcake shop. It's pronounced like the bean.

5'7" * Right-handed * Green eyes * Blonde hair

HUGH BOFF

The barista. It's actually really funny because his dad wanted him to be a barrister.

5'11" * Right-handed * Brown eyes * Light brown hair

GRUB GRIFFIN

A former contestant on a TV baking show. Likes hanging around cakes in case someone recognises him.

5'5" * Left-handed * Brown eyes * Grey hair

LOCATIONS

THE GARDEN
OUTDOORS
A beautiful court-yard with flowers. Unfortunately, overrun with wasps.

THE COFFEE ZONE
INDOORS
Where you can add your sugar and milk. Consequently, a swamp of milky sugar.

THE TOILET
INDOORS
They have the really fancy hand soap. The kind that makes you smell of dark wood and money.

WEAPONS

THE CHOCOLATE SPRINKLER
MEDIUM-WEIGHT
A particularly robust example of the genre.

A CAKE SLICE
MEDIUM-WEIGHT
For slicing cakes. But would work for people too.

A BOTTLE OF KOMBUCHA
MEDIUM-WEIGHT
Great for your gut health, not so good for your head health.

CLUES & EVIDENCE:

- Charlotte Myng was furious that someone had brought their own kombucha.
- The kombucha had really attracted the wasps.
- Hugh Boff's shirt cuffs were stained with sugary milk.
- The cake slice was in the Coffee Zone.
- **The victim had what looked like a light sprinkling of chocolate on them.**

		SUSPECTS			LOCATIONS		
		Charlotte	Hugh	Grub	Garden	Coffee zone	Toilet
WEAPONS	Sprinkler						
	Cake slice						
	Kombucha						
LOCATIONS	Garden						
	Coffee zone						
	Toilet						

WHO?

WHAT?

WHERE?

34 – MURDER AT THE ZOO

Nature was savage, red in tooth and claw. And it seemed the zoo was no exception. As they arrived, they could hear the monkeys shrieking in alarm.

SUSPECTS

SENIOR ZOOKEEPER MIKE PENNY

A huge bearlike man who would do anything to keep his animals safe.

6'5" * Right-handed * Blue eyes * Brown hair

ERIC CHALFONT

A retired schoolteacher who likes to come and talk at people as they look at the animals.

5'8" * Right-handed * Brown eyes * Grey hair

MIRA HANDLE

A zoology student who is really not too sure about the morality of zoos.

5'5" * Left-handed * Brown eyes * Brown hair

LOCATIONS

THE REPTILE ROOM
OUTDOORS
A genuinely strange musky smell in here.

THE ZOO CAFÉ
INDOORS
A school group were just here. Humans and cut-up vegetables everywhere.

THE GIFTSHOP
INDOORS
Very much over-indexing on the charismatic mega-mammal soft toys. Not much krill.

WEAPONS

A RHINO HORN
HEAVYWEIGHT
The rhino died of natural causes. The same can't be said of the victim.

A ZEBRA PEN
LIGHTWEIGHT
Stainless steel. With enough force applied...

A SELFIE STICK
MEDIUM-WEIGHT
Originally left in lost property and sturdy enough to kill.

CLUES & EVIDENCE

- Are rhino horns meant to smell like that?
- Mira Handle objects to cafés as a point of principle and will not set foot in one.
- Mike Penny very much admired the zebra pen when he saw someone had brought it.
- Tests revealed the selfie stick was wielded by someone left-handed.
- **A cuddly walrus had fallen onto the victim's body.**

		SUSPECTS			LOCATIONS		
		Mike	Eric	Mira	Reptile room	Café	Giftshop
WEAPONS	Rhino horn						
	Zebra pen						
	Selfie stick						
LOCATIONS	Reptile room						
	Café						
	Giftshop						

WHO?

WHAT?

WHERE?

35 – KILLER, DUDE!

A deathly hush hangs over Flushingham Skatepark. Onlookers are shaking their heads. 'This is so totally, totally, not sick, man.'

SUSPECTS

TONY HAWKINGS

Was really into skateboarding when he was younger, but that was quite a long time ago now...

5'9" * Right-handed * Brown eyes * Brown hair

ANYA DEV

A member of the local neighbourhood watch. She keeps her eyes on the skatepark, which she believes to be a hotbed of anti-social behaviour.

5'5" * Left-handed * Brown eyes * Red hair

HANNAH TWIST

Making a documentary about skateboard culture: *From Berks and Bucks.*

5'6" * Right-handed * Blue eyes * Dark brown hair

LOCATIONS

THE HALF-PIPE
OUTDOORS
Coated with a thin dust of skateboard wheel.

THE RAIL
INDOORS
Splinters of broken skateboard abound.

BMX RAMP
INDOORS
Covered in recently painted graffiti.

WEAPONS

A BRAND-NEW SKATEBOARD
MEDIUM-WEIGHT
Mint condition and capable of doing serious damage.

A SPANNER
LIGHTWEIGHT
Used for tightening bolts – and loosening someone's grip on life?

A BROKEN BREEZE BLOCK
MEDIUM-WEIGHT
Though broken, still heavy enough to kill someone.

CLUES & EVIDENCE:

- The breeze block was either brought by Hannah Twist or was found with splinters of skateboard near it.
- Anya Dev hadn't been brave enough to talk to whoever did bring the breeze block.
- The spanner was definitely not by the BMX ramp.
- Hannah Twist had brought her own skateboard to try and fit in.
- **The body was covered in dust from skateboard wheels.**

		SUSPECTS			LOCATIONS		
		Tony	Anya	Hannah	Half-pipe	Rail	Ramp
WEAPONS	Board						
	Spanner						
	Block						
LOCATIONS	Half-pipe						
	Rail						
	Ramp						

WHO?

WHAT?

WHERE?

36 – A (TOOTH) BRUSH WITH DEATH

The wails of the police cars intermingled with the whine of the drills in an unholy symphony of human misery. Detective Crapper didn't like visiting the dentist at the best of times.

SUSPECTS

ROGER DENTINE

Senior dentist. Teeth as white and pure as fresh winter snow. And eyes just as cold.

5'8" * Left-handed * Blue eyes * White hair

CHLOE FINCH

One of the dental nurses. Can't abide people making a fuss.

5'6" * Left-handed * Brown eyes * Brown hair

DAVE QUINCE

He hasn't been to the dentist in 27 years. He knew it was a bad idea.

5'8" * Right-handed * Brown * Grey hair

LOCATIONS

THE HYGIENIST ROOM
INDOORS
Where teeth are cleaned to within an inch of their life. The most minty fresh room in the world.

THE X-RAY ROOM
INDOORS
This is where they take a picture of your teeth to see which ones they need to put fillings into.

THE WAITING ROOM
INDOORS
A wide variety of magazines are available.

WEAPONS

NITROUS OXIDE
MEDIUM-WEIGHT
First you laugh. Then you die.

A DENTAL PROBE
LIGHTWEIGHT
Wickedly sharp and very shiny.

A DOOR STOP
MEDIUM-WEIGHT
Heavy enough to kill with.

CLUES & EVIDENCE:

- The door stop smells of spearmint.
- Chloe Finch went to dental college with the nephew of the person who brought the dental probe.
- Roger Dentine is medically unable to do X-rays for the next year, after taking too much radiation.
- Dave Quince had filled in a personality test in a magazine, using his real name.
- **Witnesses say they heard the victim laughing uproariously before they died.**

		SUSPECTS			LOCATIONS		
		Roger	Chloe	Dave	Hygienist	X-ray	Waiting
WEAPONS	Nitrous						
	Probe						
	Doorstop						

		Roger	Chloe	Dave
LOCATIONS	Hygienist			
	X-ray			
	Waiting			

WHO? ____________

WHAT? ____________

WHERE? ____________

37– A KILLER DEAL

Detective Crapper didn't know if the murder statistics among estate agents was higher than average. He rather suspected it might be.

SUSPECTS

DEAN FAST

The employee of the month at Flushingham Estates for the last 36 months. Very gelled hair.
5'8" * Right-handed * Brown eyes * Brown hair

PENNY BISCUITS

Looking to downsize.
5'7" * Left-handed * Blue eyes * Grey hair

SIMON UNCLES

The property expert for the local newspaper. Rumours are he will write favourably for money.
5' 11" * Left-handed * Green eyes * Grey hair

LOCATIONS

THE BACK OFFICE
INDOORS
Where they keep the whiteboard with sales and commission on it.

THE FRONT OFFICE
INDOORS
Where all the pictures of nice houses they don't show you are. And lots of bottles of sparkling water.

THE CAR PARK
OUTDOORS
They all drove cars with the estate agent logo on them.

WEAPONS

A BOX CUTTER
MEDIUM-WEIGHT
Used to open parcels. And people?

A FOR SALE SIGN
HEAVYWEIGHT
Definitely heavy enough to kill someone.

A BOTTLE OF PROSECCO
MEDIUM-WEIGHT
Used to celebrate the medium-sized deals.

CLUES & EVIDENCE:

- Simon Uncles once accidentally went on holiday with the person who brought the for sale sign.
- Dean Fast always opened the parcels. Everyone else did it too slowly.
- The For Sale sign was brand new and had never been outside.
- Either Simon Uncles had been in the car park or Dean Fast was in the back office.
- **The body was leant against a photo of a beautiful open-plan living space with excellent transport links.**

		SUSPECTS			LOCATIONS		
		Dean	Penny	Simon	Back	Front	Car park
WEAPONS	Box cutter						
	For Sale sign						
	Prosecco						
LOCATIONS	Back						
	Front						
	Car park						

WHO?

WHAT?

WHERE?

38 – YOU CAN'T TAKE IT WITH YOU

Charity shops always had a tinge of death about them. But this one had a lot more than most.

SUSPECTS

FRANCIS WATERBATH

A retired stockbroker who now volunteers at the shop and has very strong feelings about people who don't wash and carefully fold the clothes they donate.

5'8" * Right-handed * Blue eyes * Bald

JAZZ PICKLE

A local theatre director who sources all his costumes here.

5'3" * Left-handed * Brown eyes * Black hair

FRED PIE

He's on probation to be taken on as a proper volunteer. Keeps falling asleep in the changing room.

5'8" * Right-handed* Green eyes * White hair

LOCATIONS

DROP-OFF POINT

OUTDOORS

Out back where people drop off donations. A landscape of binbags and musty clothes.

THE BOOK SECTION

INDOORS

Mostly full of novelty books for Christmas that no-one has read. If you can imagine that.

THE COUNTER

INDOORS

Despite the clear 'no biscuits' rule, somehow there are always biscuit crumbs here.

WEAPONS

A WOODEN COAT HANGER
MEDIUM-WEIGHT
More durable than the plastic and metal ones. More deadly too.

A SAFETY PIN
LIGHTWEIGHT
Used to put the price labels on. Surely too small to kill someone?

A GRAVY BOAT
MEDIUM-WEIGHT
Someone's beloved heirloom. Now potentially a murder weapon.

CLUES & EVIDENCE

- It has been made very clear that Fred Pie is not yet qualified to take in collections. He dare not show his face there.
- Jazz Pickle knew the niece of the person who brought the gravy boat.
- The wooden hanger had been left resting on a copy of a memoir by a reality TV star.
- Despite his preference for clean clothes, Francis was covered in crumbs.
- **The forensic team said the wounds that killed the victim were the smallest they'd ever seen.**

		SUSPECTS			LOCATIONS		
		Francis	Jazz	Fred	Drop-off	Book	Counter
WEAPONS	Hanger						
	Pin						
	Boat						
LOCATIONS	Drop-off						
	Book						
	Counter						

WHO?

WHAT?

WHERE?

39 – YOUR BATTERY'S DEAD, MATE

Detective Crapper had always suspected that mechanics got away with murder, but when the call came that a body had been found at Flushingam Automotive Services, he rushed into action.

SUSPECTS

STEVE MOUSE
The owner of the garage. He winced for a living.
5'7" * Right-handed * Blue eyes * Grey hair

NICOLAS TENDON
A local classic car enthusiast who had brought 'Martha' in for a service.
5'8" * Right-handed * Brown eyes * Grey hair

MORRIS BUNYARD
He kept the garage tidy and helped moved heavy things.
6'4" * Right-handed * Blue eyes * Brown hair

LOCATIONS

THE PIT
INDOORS
So they can get under the car. Soaked in dirty oil.

THE OFFICE
INDOORS
Where they eat their fry-ups. Covered in egg and beans.

THE LOBBY
INDOORS
Where people wait while they add more zeroes to the bill. Smells strongly of pine cleaning fluid.

WEAPONS

A HEAVY WRENCH
HEAVYWEIGHT
Does exactly what it says on the tin.

A LIGHT WRENCH
LIGHTWEIGHT
You can probably work it out.

AN OLD EXHAUST PIPE
MEDIUM-WEIGHT
Caked with black sediment from the exhaust gases.

CLUES & EVIDENCE:

- Steve Mouse has the same bookie as the person who brought the exhaust pipe.
- The exhaust pipe was slick with oil.
- Nicolas Tendon seems to have somehow got dried egg on himself.
- The light wrench was only really useful as a paperweight for invoices.
- **The body smelled of pine cleaning fluid.**

		SUSPECTS			LOCATIONS		
		Steve	Nicolas	Morris	Pit	Office	Lobby
WEAPONS	Heavy						
	Light						
	Exhaust pipe						
LOCATIONS	Pit						
	Office						
	Lobby						

WHO?

WHAT?

WHERE?

40 – WHAT A WASTE

'Our concept is zero waste, so no packaging on anything.' 'Right,' said Detective Crapper. 'So it costs more and I don't get any packaging.' He shook his head. 'Nevermind, just take me to the body.'

SUSPECTS

TITUS GLIMP

Part-owner of the shop and a vocal member of the Flushingham Environmental Alliance.

5'9" * Left-handed * Blue * Blond hair

RICHARD PUNCH

A spy from the local greengrocers trying to work out how they can get away with charging twice as much for their potatoes as him.

5'9" * Right-handed * Brown eyes * Grey hair

GIL HEMON

He comes here to buy his lentils. He likes lentils.

5'11" * Right-handed * Brown eyes * Brown hair

LOCATIONS

BREAKFAST CEREALS
INDOORS
All the old favourites but not in boxes.

VEGETABLES
INDOORS
All with the soil left on so you know they've been in the ground.

CLEANING
INDOORS
Natural and organic cleaning products for you to decant into your own bottles.

WEAPONS

A LARGE TURNIP
HEAVYWEIGHT
It's a really big one.

A STORAGE BOX
MEDIUM-WEIGHT
Heavy, square and glass. Will save the planet, but not a person.

A PARING KNIFE
LIGHTWEIGHT
Used to cut vegetables free from their bunches but could kill.

CLUES & EVIDENCE:

- The paring knife had a cornflake stuck to it.
- Richard Punch's kids go to the same school as the person who brought the storage case.
- Titus Glimp loves vegetables in principle but can't bear going near actual soil.
- Gil Hemon had slipped on some organic washing-up liquid.
- **The victim died after being hit by something vaguely spherical.**

		SUSPECTS			LOCATIONS		
		Titus	Richard	Gill	Cereals	Vegetables	Cleaning
WEAPONS	Turnip						
	Box						
	Knife						
LOCATIONS	Cereals						
	Vegetables						
	Cleaning						

WHO?

WHAT?

WHERE?

No s**t, Sherlock

SECURITY CLEARANCE: THE GODFARTER

41 – POP UP, POP YOUR CLOGS

Detective Crapper is called to a new pop-up street food venue called Flushingham Boxes. Detective Crapper wonders when absolutely everyone got a tattoo, then feels very old.

SUSPECTS

BLAKE CHIMNEY

An influencer and model. He wouldn't necessarily describe himself as a foodie but others have.

6'1" * Left-handed * Dark brown eyes * Dark brown hair

BRETT HUGHES

He's here on a stag-do, but he can't seem to find the lads and no-one is picking up their phone. Weird.

5'5" * Blue eyes * Right-handed * Light brown hair

FIZZ ROWE

Is about to appear on a nationwide cooking show, so is here for inspiration.

5'9" * Green eyes * Right-handed * Blonde hair

LOCATIONS

THE CREPERIE
OUTDOORS
French snacks. Melted cheese everywhere.

INDIAN STREET FOOD
OUTDOORS
Delicious spicy smells.

THE VIP TOILET
OUTDOORS
If you pay extra, you can get access to the fancy toilet, with the proper toilet paper and luxury hand soap.

WEAPONS

CHOPSTICKS
LIGHTWEIGHT
Made from sustainably sourced bamboo but certainly strong enough to bludgeon someone.

A PIZZA SLICE
LIGHTWEIGHT
Sharp enough to cut through sourdough and human flesh. (Not at the same time)

A BOTTLE OF ORANGE WINE
HEAVYWEIGHT
A blend of hibiscus and citrus on the nose. And deadly on the head.

CLUES & EVIDENCE:

- The pizza slice was found nestled among triple-quilted toilet paper.
- The chopsticks were 100 per cent not in the creperie.
- Fizz Rowe didn't get good vibes from the suspect who brought the pizza slice.
- The chopsticks were engraved 'Smithy's Stag-do'.
- **The body has traces of gruyere on it.**

		SUSPECTS			LOCATIONS		
		Blake	Brett	Fizz	Creperie	Street food	Toilet
WEAPONS	Chopsticks						
	Pizza slice						
	Bottle of wine						
LOCATIONS	Creperie						
	Street food						
	Toilet						

WHO?

WHAT?

WHERE?

42 – NO RUNNING, NO DIVING, NO MURDER

Detective Crapper had always felt a deep sense of dread when he smelled chlorine, ever since school swimming lessons. But this morning, that feeling was especially strong.

SUSPECTS

MELISSA BUNCH

She swims 100 lengths every morning. And tells everyone about it.

5'4" * Right-handed * Brown eyes * Grey hair

BRETT CHUMP

He mainly comes to smile at the women who work in the café.

5'8" * Left-handed * Blue eyes * Bald

GIFFORD CHEYNEY

Since he retired, he has been training for an Ironman.

5'10" * Right-handed* Grey eyes * Grey hair

LOCATIONS

THE OUTDOOR POOL
OUTDOORS
Only a brave or foolhardy few are normally there as it's unheated.

THE INDOOR POOL
INDOORS
Much warmer but much fuller of toddlers who are weeing.

THE CHANGING ROOMS
INDOORS
Consider it a win if you get through here without someone else's plaster stuck to your foot.

WEAPONS

A DIVING WEIGHT
MEDIUM-WEIGHT
For lifesavers to practise with but may have been used to take a life.

A SWIMMING HOOK
Originally used to fish drowning punters out of the pool but hasn't been used for years.

A DEFIBRILLATOR
Can restart a heart, or stop it if misused.

CLUES & EVIDENCE:

- Gifford Cheyney has a dicky ticker and can't go in water that's too cold.
- Brett Chump once saw the person who brought the defibrillator on the bus.
- The diving weight had been in warm water.
- The defibrillator had a plaster stuck to the bottom of it.
- **The murder weapon had a curved edge.**

		SUSPECTS			LOCATIONS		
		Melissa	Brett	Gifford	Outdoor	Indoor	Changing
WEAPONS	Weight						
	Hook						
	Defib						
LOCATIONS	Outdoor						
	Indoor						
	Changing						

WHO?

WHAT?

WHERE?

43 – FUNERAL BLUES

That night, Detective Crapper is called to the local music venue. Someone had clearly taken their killer solos too far.

SUSPECTS

NIBS NORTON

A legendary promotor on the Flushingham music scene. He discovered The Dingwalls, Josh Git *and* Fruity Johnson.

6'2" * Right-handed * Blue eyes * Blonde hair

BURT WIG

A long in the tooth jazz drummer who likes to give advice to up-and-coming artists in the area.

5'10" * Right-handed * Brown eyes * Brown hair

JENNY RUTHERS

The music correspondent for the *Flushingham Gazette*. A good review from her can make a band. And vice versa.

5'7" * Left-handed * Blue eyes * Brown hair

LOCATIONS

BACKSTAGE
INDOORS
Slightly worse for wear. Looks like it hasn't been dusted since a young Mick Jagger did it.

THE BAR
INDOORS
Dead classy. They've got olives and everything.

THE STEPS
OUTDOORS
A steep flight of steps down to the basement venue.

WEAPONS

A DRUM STICK
LIGHTWEIGHT
Made for hitting things hard.

A MICROPHONE
MEDIUM-WEIGHT
The manufacturers don't advise it, but you could hit someone with it.

A BOTTLE OF BOURBON
MEDIUM-WEIGHT
It would be a waste of bourbon but could certainly scramble somebody's brain.

CLUES & EVIDENCE:

- Nibs Norton had once toured Nuneaton with the uncle of the person who'd brought the drum stick.
- Burt Wig had been telling everyone to be careful with his microphone.
- The bottle of bourbon wasn't in its natural home behind the bar.
- Jenny Ruthers was seen by multiple passers-by making a phone call on the steps.
- **When the body was moved, it left an outline in the thick layer of dust underneath it.**

		SUSPECTS			LOCATIONS		
		Nibs	Burt	Jenny	Backstage	Bar	Steps
WEAPONS	Drum stick						
	Mic						
	Bourbon						
LOCATIONS	Backstage						
	Bar						
	Steps						

WHO?

WHAT?

WHERE?

44 – TILL DEATH US DO PART

There were weddings and there were funerals, and Detective Crapper was of the opinion that you shouldn't mix the two – not only because of the colour schemes.

SUSPECTS

PENNY MONCRIEF

The mother of the bride. Half-human, half-sofa.

5'6" * Left-handed * Blue eyes * Grey hair.

MITCHELL BONER

The best man. His speech made several people cry and not in a good way.

5'9" * Right-handed * Brown eyes * Blond hair

REVEREND FLAPS

The vicar for the ceremony. He takes a very dim view of happy couples writing their own vows.

5'11" * Right-handed * Brown eyes * Brown hair

LOCATIONS

THE OUTSIDE STEPS

OUTSIDE

Where the couples come out. Still covered in confetti.

THE KITCHEN

INDOORS

Where the wedding feasts are made. Though there probably won't be one tonight.

THE VOWS ROOM

INDOORS

Full of beautiful white flowers with yellow pollen.

WEAPONS

A BIBLE
HEAVYWEIGHT
Leather-bound and with the heft of centuries.

A KNIFE SHARPENER
MEDIUM-WEIGHT
A heavy metal rod covered in metallic dust from sharpened knives.

A SERVING PLATE OF NIBBLES
MEDIUM-WEIGHT
For the post-wedding drinks. But perfectly serviceable as a murder weapon.

CLUES & EVIDENCE:

- Either Reverend Flaps brough the nibble plate, is the owner of the knife, or it was in the kitchen.
- Mitchell had winked at the person who had brought the plate of nibbles.
- The knife sharpener wasn't found in the Vows Room.
- 'Guv, I know you tell me to check my assumptions but I was right about who brought the Bible.'
- **The body had little scraps of paper stuck to it with blood.**

		SUSPECTS			LOCATIONS		
		Penny	Mitchell	Reverend	Steps	Kitchen	Vows
WEAPONS	Bible						
	Sharpener						
	Plate						
LOCATIONS	Steps						
	Kitchen						
	Vows						

WHO?

WHAT?

WHERE?

45 – DEATH ON THE BIG SCREEN

The first thing they needed to do was work out if this was murder or whether someone had just had a heart attack when they saw how much a ticket, a medium drink and a medium popcorn cost. Round these parts that was essentially natural causes.

SUSPECTS

PROJECTIONIST BEN FLOAT

Detective Crapper assumed they were all digital and automatic now, but apparently not.

5'11" * Left-handed * Hazel eyes * Brown hair

HADRIAN CABBAGE

Has been to see the new superhero movie 12 times already and is watching it again today.

5'6" * Right-handed * Green eyes * Blond hair

CLEM TWITTING

He likes to hang out at the cinema and read books by French people. One day he hopes someone will strike up a conversation.

5'7" * Right-handed * Brown eyes * Black hair

LOCATIONS

THE POPCORN COUNTER
INDOORS
A carpet of popcorn awaits you.

THE SWEETY ZONE
INDOORS
What used to be penny sweets but should now be called several pounds sweets.

THE DRINK MACHINE
INDOORS
Where people fill their own drinks. Surrounded by melted ice and syrup.

WEAPONS

A TORCH
LIGHTWEIGHT
Broken now. Used to guide people to their seats or check whether they were up to no good in the darkness.

A CANNISTER OF POPCORN BUTTER
HEAVYWEIGHT
Heavy enough to put the lights out permanently.

A WALKING STICK
MEDIUM-WEIGHT
Left in lost property.

CLUES & EVIDENCE:

- The walking stick has tiny pieces of popcorn on it.
- Hadrian Cabbage noticed someone carrying the cannister of popcorn butter past him.
- Projectionist Ben has a phobia of tiny fruit made of sugar. It's so rare there isn't even a Latin name for it.
- Clem Twitting's feet kept sticking to the floor.
- **There was broken glass on the body.**

		SUSPECTS			LOCATIONS		
		Ben	Hadrian	Clem	Popcorn	Sweeties	Drinks
WEAPONS	Torch						
	Popcorn butter						
	Walking stick						
LOCATIONS	Popcorn						
	Sweeties						
	Drinks						

WHO?

WHAT?

WHERE?

46 – A MURDER MYSTERY

'We meet on the third Thursday of the month and take it in turns to pick the book. But this time it all went very wrong.' Detective Crapper had witnessed some pretty fierce altercations in his own book group. Who had gone too far here?

SUSPECTS

LILLIAN FILBERT

She studied literature under the dreaming spires of Oxford and isn't afraid to tell you.

5'5" * Left-handed * Green eyes * Brown hair

JILL BISTO

She has ambitions to write her own series of thrillers set in the world of dentistry.

5'2" * Right-handed * Brown eyes * Blonde hair

JUDE SMUDGE

He's a poet, really, but does write some fiction.

5'11" * Left-handed * Brown eyes * Black hair

LOCATIONS

THE KITCHEN

INDOORS

Where people could make themselves cups of tea and coffee. A thin layer of instant coffee granules was on most surfaces.

THE CORRIDOR

INDOORS

A timetable was up on the wall, showing which groups used the community hall on which days.

THE STOREROOM

INDOORS

Mainly used to keep lost property, including an odd variety of single shoes.

WEAPONS

A STATUE OF A DOG
HEAVYWEIGHT
Made by one of the pottery classes. A bit crumbly and wonky.

A WALKIE-TALKIE
MEDIUM-WEIGHT
Left in a cupboard by a security guard.

BICYCLE PUMP
LIGHTWEIGHT
Used to add air to tyres and perhaps remove it from lungs.

CLUES & EVIDENCE:

- Jude Smudge went to school with the son of the person who brought the walkie-talkie.
- Lillian Filbert has the key to the pottery room.
- The walkie-talkie was definitely not in the storeroom.
- Either Jude Smudge was in the storeroom or Lillian Filbert was in the kitchen.
- **There were fragments of clay found on the body.**

		SUSPECTS			LOCATIONS		
		Lillian	Jill	Jude	Kitchen	Corridor	Storeroom
WEAPONS	Statue						
	Walkie-talkie						
	Pump						
LOCATIONS	Kitchen						
	Corridor						
	Storeroom						

WHO? ____________

WHAT? ____________

WHERE? ____________

47 – KILLER INK

Detective Crapper had never got a tattoo because he'd never been able to think of anything he liked enough to want on his body forever (except for solving murders, and that was quite hard to represent as an image).

SUSPECTS

SCRATCH JOHNSON

The owner of Flushingham Tatz. A perfectionist.
5'8" * Right-handed * Brown eyes * Black hair

POPPY HOLD

The tattoo parlour's expert in piercing. Her eyes say she has seen things most mortals could never comprehend.
5'8" * Left-handed * Brown eyes * Black hair

JOSH WILLIAMS

He was thinking, *Maybe a leaf, or a feather, or, like, two parallel lines, or maybe a dolphin, or, like, what's Arabic for love and wisdom?*
5'8" * Right-handed * Green eyes * Blond

LOCATIONS

THE DESIGN CORNER
INDOORS
Where the book of designs is kept.

THE TATTOO CHAIR
INDOORS
Sprayed with antiseptic. You can't be too careful.

THE WAITING AREA
INDOORS
Does Detective Crapper imagine it, or can you actually see the nervous sweat on the surfaces?

WEAPONS

A JEWELLED SKULL
MEDIUM-WEIGHT
Definitely hard enough to break the non-jewelled kind.

A TATTOO NEEDLE
MEDIUM-WEIGHT
Still with traces of ink on it.

A MOP
Used to clean the floor.

CLUES & EVIDENCE:

- The book of designs is guarded by Skully McSkullface.
- They're so hygienic, even the handle of their mop smells of strong disinfectant.
- The lab says it's certain the killer was left-handed.
- Scratch Johnson was in the design corner all day.
- **There was tattoo ink in the victim's death wound.**

		SUSPECTS			LOCATIONS		
		Scratch	Poppy	Josh	Design	Tattoo	Waiting
WEAPONS	Skull						
	Needle						
	Mop						
LOCATIONS	Design						
	Tattoo						
	Waiting						

WHO?

WHAT?

WHERE?

48 – DEATH BY CHOCOLATE

After all that darkness, Detective Crapper found it a relief to go somewhere a little bit lighter. But even here at Cocoa MG, death followed him. Everyone knew too many sweet things weren't good for you. But this was taking things too far.

SUSPECTS

RENEE BUFFET

The mercurial chocolatier behind innovative new flavours like leek and parmesan and gravy chocolate.

5'9" * Right-handed * Brown eyes * Black hair

REG TREMBLY

Often heard to say, 'It's ridiculous to say chocolate is addictive. I can stop whenever I want. I just don't want to.'

5'8" * Right-handed * Brown eyes * Grey hair

JOHN SMITH

An agent from a nationwide chocolate manufacturer, here to try and work out what all the fuss is about (and steal all their ideas).

5'10" * Left-handed * Blue eyes (dark glasses) * What looks like a blond wig

LOCATIONS

THE HOT CHOCOLATE BAR
INDOORS
They have 42 options.

THE FLAVOUR MACHINE
INDOORS
Here you answer a series of questions about flavours you like and they create a personalised chocolate selection box.

THE TASTING BOOTH
INDOORS
A soundproofed and entirely dark room, allowing you to concentrate on the flavour of the chocolate. Very hard to clean, so covered in chocolate crumbs.

WEAPONS

A SACK OF CACAO
HEAVYWEIGHT
Organic, fair trade and heavy enough to kill.

A KITCHEN KNIFE
MEDIUM-WEIGHT
Used to cut chocolate and possibly the victim.

A BOTTLE OF LIQUEUR
One of the ingredients for the chocolates.

CLUES & EVIDENCE:

- Renee Buffet is not a fan of the flavour machine, but the money men made him have it. He will never go near it.
- Reg Trembly is claustrophobic and scared of the dark.
- John Smith was worried the suspect who brought the liqueur bottle knew who he really was, so found somewhere dark to hide.
- The kitchen knife was inscribed with the words 'Chocolate Maestro'.
- **The body had several cacao nibs on it.**

		SUSPECTS			LOCATIONS		
		Renee	Reg	John	Hot chocolate	Flavour machine	Tasting booth
WEAPONS	Sack						
	Knife						
	Bottle						
LOCATIONS	Hot chocolate						
	Flavour machine						
	Tasting booth						

WHO?

WHAT?

WHERE?

49 – DEATH IN MINIATURE

Every time Detective Crapper thought he might get a rest, a new call came in. This time to Flushingham's model village. Every building they'd ever visited was laid out before them in miniature including the location of every murder they'd ever investigated. Perhaps if Detective Crapper looked closely enough, he'd see a tiny Detective Crapper trying to solve them.

SUSPECTS

ALABASTER SNARK

The owner of the model village and a mysterious recluse.
5'6" * Right-handed * Blue eyes * White hair

FRED QUIMBY

One of the volunteers who maintains the model village. Passionate about miniatures.
5'7" * Left-handed * Brown eyes * White hair

GLEN BISHOP

He has visited every model village in the country. This is the first time there's been a murder.
5'9" * Right-handed * Green eyes * Red hair

LOCATIONS

THE COAST
OUTDOORS
The beaches are made with regular sand, which means the grains must be giant to the tiny people.

THE CITY CENTRE
OUTDOORS
The detail is incredible – tiny graffiti, tiny traffic jams, tiny dog poos.

E TOILETS
INDOORS
These are regular sized.

WEAPONS

A MODEL TRAIN
MEDIUM-WEIGHT
Could be used as a cudgel.

A CHURCH SPIRE
MEDIUM-WEIGHT
A fearsome point to it.

A KETTLE
MEDIUM-WEIGHT
One of the old-fashioned ones that sits on a stove top. Full of scaley water.

CLUES & EVIDENCE:

- Under a magnifying glass was a tiny dog poo on the tip of the church spire.
- Fred Quimby is the same star sign as the person who brought the model train.
- Glen Bishop has a phobia of public toilets and hasn't been in one since 1992.
- Alabaster Stark was holding the church spire.
- **The body had limescale on it.**

		SUSPECTS: Alabaster	SUSPECTS: Fred	SUSPECTS: Glen	LOCATIONS: Coast	LOCATIONS: City centre	LOCATIONS: Toilet
WEAPONS	Train						
WEAPONS	Spire						
WEAPONS	Kettle						
LOCATIONS	Coast						
LOCATIONS	City centre						
LOCATIONS	Toilet						

WHO?

WHAT?

WHERE?

50 – EXIT, STAGE DEATH

It was the opening night of the starry new production of *Hamlet*. But there was one more death than was traditional. During the interval, a body had been found. The Chief of Police was in the audience, along with every important person in Flushingam. Never had the pressure been greater on Detective Crapper.

SUSPECTS

SIR PERCIVAL FLUSHING

The descendant of the founder of Flushingham. A patron of all arts but especially the theatre.

5'8" * Right-handed * Blue eyes * White hair

JASPER GIMLET

One of the ushers at the theatre. Clearly goes to the gym a lot.

5'6" * Right-handed * Green eyes * Blonde hair

ARTY FROIM

The director of the play. He looks inconsolable.

5'6" * Left-handed * Brown eyes * Dark brown hair

LOCATIONS

THE BAR
INDOORS
They had already started pouring out the intermission champagne.

THE STAGE
INDOORS
Covered in mounds of mud.

BACKSTAGE
INDOORS
A spot where the actors reapply their make-up.

WEAPONS

A STAGE DAGGER
LIGHTWEIGHT
Also works in real life.

A STAGE WEIGHT
HEAVYWEIGHT
Used to weigh down part of the set. If you were strong, you could lift it.

A THERMOS FLASK
HEAVYWEIGHT
Used to keep Hamlet's coffee warm till the interval.

CLUES & EVIDENCE:

- The dagger has mud all over it.
- Sir Percival is a hard-line teetotaller and refuses to even be near alcohol.
- Arty Froim doesn't concern himself with things like stage weights. He would never even touch one.
- Jasper Gimlet has somehow got traces of make-up on his sleeves.
- **The body had splashes of coffee on it.**

		SUSPECTS			LOCATIONS		
		Percival	Jasper	Arty	Bar	Stage	Backstage
WEAPONS	Dagger						
	Weight						
	Flask						
LOCATIONS	Bar						
	Stage						
	Backstage						

WHO?

WHAT?

WHERE?

EXTRA CLUES

1. Someone had left a note written on one of the menus. It said, 'You should know, in the place where the bosses sit, they found a load of disgusting healthy drinks'.

2. Left scrawled on one of the receipt rolls were the words, 'Remember the good old days when soup was old-fashioned British soup? I refuse to buy that modern tofu wokerati rubbish.'

3. 'Testing, testing, one, two, three. Has anyone seen Carinna, the guitarist from Vegetable Matters?'

4. As Detective Crapper tours the grounds, he hears a psst from the bushes. 'Gerrard Van De Borre is a keen tenpin bowler, you know.'

5. 'Oh, the only way he can wind down after a dinner service is to steam his stress away,' said the first officer.

6. Preliminary tests reveal that the statue of the toilet brush was scratched with gravel.

7. Detective Crapper was told by multiple interviewees that Maestro Clive would never leave the orchestra pit (in case he saw a hanger).

8. 'It's not rocket science, is it guv,' said the constable with a tone Detective Crapper wasn't entirely sure he enjoyed. 'The barrel was in the place they store barrels.'

9. Remembering something, Detective Crapper went through the pages of his notebook and eventually found the quote he'd taken down previously: 'Little Dave goes to every fancy dress party as Boris Johnson.'

10. 'What does that look like to you, Crapper?' said the forensics chief. 'There on the frozen lamb – is that a fake moustache?'

11. 'That's exactly the sort of spade you'd need to cut through the roots of grasses up on the headland,' says a helpful man, before wandering off.

12. Simon Simonson had packing tape stuck to his shoe.

13. The broom was leant against a sign that said, 'Doors open at 9pm. No refunds.'

14. Professor Pisces' shoelaces are soaked in what smells like rotting fish guts.

15. Regina had a prescription in her pocket for the pills found in the bottle.

16. Martin Prunes was a firm believer in the healing power of the cold.

17. They used the frame to hold a filing cabinet in the back office closed.

18. Hectate Van Ducker loved the flavour of raspberry.

19. The rake was used to keep the gravel around the eco toilet neat.

20. Nick Aulait was such a perfectionist he even dried his client's hair himself.

21. Gordon Dribble had a parsley leaf stuck to him.

22. Edna Thimble has written multiple times that she never goes anywhere without her travel iron.

23. Basher Bumpkins had the sort of reed that only grows near ponds stuck to him.

24. According to medical records, Ivy Tooter has recently had a hip replacement.

25. Jim Branson was eating his lunch with the rest of the staff.

26. 'Does that sledgehammer smell of cider to you, guv?'

27. Billy Linen started his career as a zip repairman and always feels most comfortable there.

28. 'We've been able to cross-reference and work out that the coffin handle was in the display room with total certainty.'

29. Jez Bundle had already started on his socials, talking about the 'amazing big mug of coffee' he'd been served.

30. The digital notebook case was plastered with stickers for NFTs. Whatever they were.

31. The fork was seen in the background of a photograph leaning up against the gardener's hut.

32. Milton Boardwalk's book of lyrics was soaked in a mixture of old beer and cider.

33. Charlotte Myng smelled of cedar wood and expense accounts.

34. You are informed that Mike Penny was coming out of the Reptile Room when you arrived.

35. Multiple witnesses report Anya Dev had the spanner.

36. Chloe Finch was the only one who had the key to the X-ray room.

37. The For Sale sign had a smudge of whiteboard marker pen on it.

38. The safety pin had a fragment of black bin bag on it.

39. The heavy wrench smelled weirdly of pine.

40. Richard Punch was seen by witnesses rifling through the carrots.

41. Brett Hughes still smells faintly of spices.

42. The diving weight had been labelled 'GC'.

43. The microphone had an olive stone stuck to it.

44. Mitchell Boner was found to have an odd metallic dust on his hands.

45. Hadrian Cabbage was spotted by multiple witnesses next to the popcorn booth.

46. The walkie-talkie had coffee granules on it.

47. Josh Williams was seen by witnesses with the mop.

48. As well as chocolate crumbs, they also found cacao nibs in the tasting booth, which seems odd. Who's eating those raw?!

49. Glen Bishop was seen by multiple witnesses with the model train.

50. Jasper Gimlet is the only suspect strong enough to lift the stage weight.

ANSWERS

1. 'It was Mr Boom, with the kettlebell, in the Sand Pit room,' cried Detective Crapper. The influencer only started crying when he was told there'd be no wifi at the police station. 'I did it...I did it for the gram,' he sobbed to himself. 'But he said it would all work out!'

Benji Stone – Bottle of liqueur – The portaloos

Dan Daniels – Selfie stick – The site office

Mr Boom – Kettlebell – The sandpit room

2. 'It was Lucian Gadd, with the olive oil, by the bins,' said detective Crapper. 'That shirt with those trousers,' Lucian cried. 'I simply could not allow it!'

Harissa Jones – A poisoned slice of cheesecake – The self-service tills

Lucian Gadd – Olive oil – By the bins

Humbert Wilde – A tin of soup – The freezer

3. 'It was Bobo the Magnificent, with the astonishingly over-priced bottle of beer, backstage!' roared Detective Crapper.

'It's true!' cried out Bobo. 'And I'd do it again in a heartbeat. He sipped my beer without asking. That was about twenty quid of beer on its own!'

Bobo the Magnificent – Bottle of beer – Backstage

Jackson Quint – Scaffolding – The VIP tent

Carinna Vedigris - A guitar lead – Festival toilets

4. 'It was Gerrard Van De Borre with the bowling ball, in the cinema!' cried Detective Crapper. The murderer was silent as they led him away. But as he passed Crapper, he whispered 'You'll never beat him you know. He knows every move you'll make.'

Millicent Jones – Kitchen knife – Kitchen

Gerrard Van De Borre – Bowling ball – Cinema

Chad Chadson – Smartphone – The gym

5. 'It was Chef Brandywine with the hypodermic needle, on the viewing deck,' said Detective Crapper. 'Maybe the next person will think again before they say my red wine reduction is thin and lacking in unctuousness,' Brandywine sniffed.

Chief Engineer Masterson – Fake tree branch – Ship's sauna

Chef Brandywine – Hypodermic needle – The viewing deck

Harriet Ombudsman – Titanium briefcase – Sundeck

6. 'It was Professor Porcelain with the poison, in the museum lobby,' said Detective Crapper. 'Oh bravo, my boy,' said the professor smiling gently. 'And there I was thinking you wouldn't be able to solve it. Maybe our mutual friend has underestimated you.'

Professor Porcelain – Chemical vial – Museum lobby

Cynthia Boondoggle – Statue – Back garden

Bernard Custermode – Toilet lid – Storeroom

7. 'It was Henry Hamson with the sharpened triangle in the cloakroom,' said Detective Crapper. Henry Hamson was humming furiously to himself. 'We might play the instruments, Detective. But he is the conductor.' With that, he was taken away for processing.

Maestro Clive – Ethical tote bag – Orchestra pit

Henry Hamson – Triangle – The cloakroom

Margo Fitzhalligan – Sharpened violin bow – The bar

8. 'It was Dave Dave, with the barrel, in the cellar,' said Detective Crapper, who couldn't help feeling this was a particularly run of the mill case.

'At least now they might call me Murderer Dave,' said Dave Dave. At least, that's what the nice bloke I've been messaging with said.'

Big Dave – A dart – The snug

Little Dave – Poisoned pork scratching – The public bar

Dave Dave – Barrel – The cellar

9. 'Poppy Jones, with the poisoned water, in the pub,' said Detective Crapper. 'But why?' 'I had to do it,' Poppy sobbed. 'He promised he'd free the dolphins if I did. All of them. We've been messaging for months! All I had to do was put what he sent in his drink.' But before he could ask her anything else, another call came through. High priority.

TJ – Placard – Roundabout

Poppy Bannister – Poisoned water – Pub

Little Dave – Boris Johnson mask – Statue

10. 'It was Mina Jones, with the dental floss, near the lifts,' said Detective Crapper. Mina nodded quietly. 'I didn't mean for him to die,' she said finally. 'But he came at me. And if it stops his plans to sell the futures of everyone in this town to the highest bidder, it will be worth it.'

Gustav Bublet – Lamb – Fire escape

Gordon Badger – Corkscrew – Stage

Mina Jones – Dental floss – Lifts

11.'It was Bernard Collins, with the spade, on the headland,' said Detective Crapper. 'I admit it,' said Bernard. 'I've been trying to find the man who broke my bass record for years. He was right where Mr Fry said he'd be.' 'Who?' asked Detective Crapper. 'I don't know who he is, but he always signed off his emails with his full name. Mr Iota Fry.'

Bernar Collins – Spade – Headland

Bodie Doyle – Fishing line – Beach huts

Gwymethy Chalfont – Starfish – Pier

12. 'It was Penelope Bandelier with the toilet brush, out front of the shop.' 'I won't say anything without my lawyer,' said Penelope. 'Call Mr Ray Foti and tell him I need my lawyer.'

Penelope Bandolier – Toilet brush – Shop front

Simon Simonson – Receipt spike – Loading bay

Gary Chugging – Crowbar – Store room

13. 'It was Finn Gitson, with the broom in the upstairs toilet,' cried Detective Crapper. 'You can't not wash your hands,' said Finn. 'That is properly disgusting.'

Finn Gitson – Broom – Toilet

Ari Vorn – Ketchup – Chiller

Melony Baker – Knife – Carpark

14.'It was Randall Finch, with the feeding bucket, in the giftshop,' said Detective Crapper. 'I thought he was a rogue haddock, I genuinely did!' said Randall. 'That nice man Mr Fairtoy gave me his bucket to hold. And the next thing I knew I was swinging it.'

Professor Pisces – Narwhal's tusk – Penguin pool

Randall Finch – Feeding bucket – Giftshop

Gil Flapper – Pencil – Café

15. 'It was Regina Harking, with the bottle of pills, in the shooting gallery,' Said Detective Crapper. 'It's true!' screamed Regina. 'It was me. I waited till he was playing that water shooting game then put the crushed-up pills in his drink. He didn't see a thing! Will Mr Tofiary let my mother go now, do you think?'

Angelica Bandolis – Metal – Queue

Regina Harking – Bottle of pills – Shooting gallery

Greg Wu – Fence post – Arcade

16. 'It was Martin Prunes, with the weights wrapped in a towel, in the cryotherapy room,' said Detective Crapper. Martin said nothing as they led him away, just smiled with an odd look in his eye.

Hannah Plimpton – Nail scissors – Hot stones

Martin Prunes – Weight in towel – Cryotherapy

Jeb Fundament – Bottle of serum – Isolation tank

17. 'It was Timothy Chalet with the palette knife, in the gallery,' said Detective Crapper. 'It wasn't personal. It was just business,' said Timothy. 'His art just went up 1000% in value. And I have my silent partner to thank for the idea.'

Timothy Chalet – Palette knife – Gallery

Hal Harlow – Picture frame – Office

Benjamin Tiffle – Champagne bottle – Toilets

18. 'It was Sharlene Twigg, with the half brick, in the alleyway,' said Detective Crapper. 'He came in three times a week for almost three years, and not once did he say please!' said Sharlene.

Hecate Van Ducker – Pen – Counter

Sharlene Twigg – Half brick – Back alley

Miguel Bossanova – Refill – Store cupboard

19.'It was Jack Loam, with the rake by the eco toilet,' said Detective Crapper. There was a gasp.

Jack Loam – Rake – Eco toilet

Helga Omlit – Parasol weight – Seed library

Lonny Dimble – Bamboo cane – Manure corner

20. 'It was Nick Aulait, with the hair straighteners, in the hair drying zone,' said Detective Crapper. 'You give people art and they throw it back in your face,' said Nick.

Marnie Oakwell – Cutthroat razor – Perm zone

Nick Aulait – Hair straighteners – Hair-drying zone

Kris Rigg – Hairspray– Wash zone

21. 'It was Eric Bass with the knife sharpener, out back of the shop,' said Detective Crapper. Eric Bass nodded. 'There's only so much dead fish any man can take,' he said.

Eric Bass – Knife sharpener – Back of shop

Gordon Dribble – Filleting knife –Front of shop

Hortense Bechemel – Halibut – Counter

22. 'It was Geoffrey Chaffinch, with the coat hanger, in the back garden,' said Detective Crapper. 'He snored the whole night,' said Geoffrey. 'I need peace and quiet!'

Katie Beans – Bottle of sherry – Bathroom

Geoffrey Chaffinch – A coat hanger – Back garden

Edna Thimble – Travel iron – Dining room

23. 'It was Harry Balls, with the cricket box, in the pavilion,' cried Detective Crapper. The whole room shuddered. What a way to go. 'He screwed me over in a business deal. I had to,' said Harry. 'God bless Tom Friary, that's all I can say.'

Harry Balls – Cricket box – Pavilion

Basher Bumpkins – Cricket ball in a sock – Duck pond

Olivia Heathcliffe – Cricket stump – Outfield

24. 'It was Ivy Tooter with the crutch, in the lost property cupboard!' said Detective Crapper. 'It was brought to my attention by a concerned citizen named Tom Friary that they weren't the right sort and there was only one thing I could do,' said Ivy.

Hen Chickens – Tea urn – Kitchen

Ivy Tooter – Crutch – Lost property cupboard

Ben Darcy – Walking stick – Garden

25. 'It was Jim Branson with the plyers, in the canteen,' said Detective Crapper. 'He'd been hired as a spy,' said Jim. 'I couldn't let them steal my ideas. We are all part of the Tifor Army, Detective.'

Nelo Smuk – Toilet brush – Garden

Jim Branson – Plyers – Canteen

Gwen Chips – Laptop case – Ideas room

26. 'It was Jed Thrup with the antique hay rake, in the dairy,' said Detective Crapper. 'Sometimes these things can't be helped,' sniffed Jed. 'Am I allowed to bring Daisy?' he added, nodding at his rake.

Jed Thrup – Antique rake – Dairy

Felicity Melp – Sledgehammer – Orchard

Nathaniel West – Milking bucket – Old barn

27. 'It was Gladys Baines with the spare zips in the launderette zone,' said Detective Crapper. 'He was trying to convince me to buy a washing machine from his shop,' said Gladys. 'I wasn't having any of that.'

Billy Linen – Bottle of solvent – Zip zone

Gladys Baines – Spare zips – Launderette zone

Vernon Guber – Big pole – Dry-clean zone

28. 'It was Robert Ian Peters III, with the coffin handle, in the office,' said Detective Crapper. 'He said if "I did it, then I'd finally get everything I wanted," said Peters II. 'Who said that?' asked his father. 'He's a moderator for *Rift*, that online game I play. I just know him as Mayor Rift.'

Robert Ian Peters – Flower cane – Morgue

Robert Ian Peters Jr – Bottle of brandy – Display room

Robert Ian Peters III – Coffin handle – The office

29. 'It was John Bomber, with the fork, in the back alley,' said Detective Crapper. 'He used the last of the red sauce. You can't do that,' said John Bomber, 'or we're no better than animals.'

Clive Thimble – Vase of flowers – Outside tables

John Bomber – Fork – Back alley

Jez Bundle – Coffee mug – Kitchen

30. 'It was Lunar, with the data stick holder, in the café,' said Detective Crapper. Lunar nodded calmly. 'It felt exactly like he said it would. How curious,' she finally said.

Juniper Finch – Metal water cup – Hot yoga

Kurt Wobble – Digital notebook – The vaping room

Lunar – Novelty data stick holder – The café

31. 'It was Major Henry Burgers, with the trowel, in the rose garden,' said Detective Crapper. 'He had brought his own barbeque and was preparing to light it,' said the Major. 'I had no choice.'

Major Henry Burgers – Trowel – Rose garden

Hugo Dangle – Fork – Gardener's hut

Miriam Frimple – Branch – Ornamental fountain

32. 'It was Suze O'Malley with the mic stand, on stage,' roared Detective Crapper. 'I don't' know what happened,' said Suze. 'Just before I went on stage, someone came and whispered something in my ear and the next thing I remember I'm sitting here. What have I done? What have I done?!'

Suze O'Malley – Mic stand – The stage

Milton Boardwalk – Bottle of wine – The bar

Leonard Pilchard – Sword – The back row

33. 'It was Charlotte Myng, with the chocolate sprinkler in the toilet,' said Detective Crapper. 'Listen, detective,' Charlotte said. 'If you think you can make a cupcake without breaking a few eggs, you're sorely mistaken. Unless they're egg-free cupcakes, which we actually do. They're really great.'

Charlotte Myng – Chocolate sprinkler – Toilet

Hugh Boff – Cake slice – Coffee zone

Grub Griffin – Bottle of kombucha – Garden

34. 'It was Mira Handle, with the selfie stick, in the giftshop,' said Detective Crapper. 'We have no right to keep them in a cage,' said Mira. 'Let this act draw attention to it. I and the other members of the 'Mira Forty' are willing to go to prison for what we believe.'

Mike Penny – Rhino horn – Reptile house

Mira Handle – Selfie stick – Giftshop

Eric Chalfont – Zebra pen – Zoo café

35. 'It was Anya Dev, with the spanner, in the half-pipe,' said Detective Crapper. Anya looked defiant. 'You can push us so far, but no further,' she said. 'The noise, the graffiti, the laughter and cries of joy. It's insufferable. He's absolutely right, I had to do it.'

Tony Hawkings – Breeze block – Rail

Anya Dev – Spanner – Halfpipe

Hannah Twist – Skateboard – BMX ramp

36. 'It was Chloe Finch, with the nitrous oxide in the X-ray room,' said Detective Crapper. Chloe Finch caught his eye. 'When a tooth is rotten, Detective, we take it out. He taught me that.'

Roger Dentine – Door stop – Hygienist room

Chloe Finch – Nitrous oxide – X-ray room

Dave Quince – Dental probe – Waiting room

37. 'It was Dean Fast, with the box cutter, in the front office,' said Detective Crapper. 'I'm number one here,' said Dean Fast. 'It's like my favourite podcaster Timor Fray says, 'To succeed in business, you have to be a killer".'

Dean Fast – Box cutter – Front office

Penny Biscuits – For Sale sign – Back office

Simon Uncles – Prosecco bottle – Car park

38. 'It was Jazz Pickle, with the safety pin, at the drop-off point,' said Detective Crapper. 'He gave the Flushingam Players the worst review we've ever had,' cried Jazz Pickle. 'I was tipped off he came here. It was just a matter of time.'

Francis Waterbath – Gravy boat – Counter

Jazz Pickle – Safety pin – Drop-off point

Fred Pie – Coat hanger – Book section

39. 'It was Steve Mouse, with the heavy wrench in the lobby,' said Detective Crapper. 'Listen,' said Steve Mouse. 'I'm not saying a word till I talk to my lawyer. Someone give Mr Toifray a ring.'

Steve Mouse – Heavy wrench – Lobby

Nicolas Tendon – Light wrench – Office

Morris Bunyard – Exhaust pipe – The pit

40. 'It was Richard Punch, with the turnip, in the vegetable section,' said Detective Crapper. 'I heard someone saying that buying vegetables like this was a revolutionary new idea and I just snapped. I'm truly sorry,' said Richard Punch.

Titus Glimp – Paring knife – Breakfasts

Richard Punch – Turnip – Vegetables

Gil Hemon – Storage box – Cleaning

41. 'It was Fizz Rowe, with the orange wine, in the creperie,' cried Detective Crapper. Fizz nodded. 'I recognised him from the audition round,' she said. 'He was amazing. I only meant to make him miss the next round, not kill him!'

Blake Chimney – Pizza slice – VIP toilet

Brett Hughes – Chopsticks – Indian street food

Fizz Rowe – Orange wine – The creperie

42. 'It was Brett Chump, with the swimming hook, in the outdoor pool,' said Detective Crapper. 'She said if I did it,' said Brett, 'then Margo at the café would be impressed.' 'Who said that, Brett?' asked Detective Crapper gently. 'That nice lady who knows my mum, Ma Frytior. We've been messaging for months.'

Melissa Bunch – Defibrillator – Changing rooms

Brett Chump – Swimming hook – Outdoor pool

Gifford Cheyney – Diving weight – Indoor pool

43. 'It was Nibs Norton, with the bottle of bourbon, backstage,' said Detective Crapper.

'Yeah, it's true!' said Nibs. 'Twenty years ago, he took my girl. So tonight, I took his life. I just wish I could buy the guy who told me he was playing tonight a drink. Never got his name, though.'

Nibs Norton – Bottle of bourbon – Backstage

Burt Wig – Microphone – The bar

Jenny Ruthers – A drumstick – The steps

44. 'It was Mitchell Boner, with the knife sharpener, on the outside steps!' said Detective Crapper. Mitchell breathed out almost in relief. 'He told me he'd have done a better job,' said Mitchell. 'He said I was a terrible best man. I just snapped. Can you call the number on this card? That nice bloke on the stag-do gave it to me. He said to call if I was ever in trouble. What was his name? Tom something... Tom Friary! That's it. Lovely bloke.'

Penny Moncrief – Plate of nibbles – Kitchen

Mitchell Boner – Knife sharpener – Outside steps

Reverend Flaps – Bible – The vows room

45. 'It was Hadrian Cabbage with the torch, in the sweety zone,' said Detective Crapper. 'Sometimes,' said Hadrian, 'sometimes we get the heroes we deserve. Together, me and my sidekick, Ort Ramify, will rescue the world from evil.'

Ben Float – Walking stick – Popcorn counter

Hadrian Cabbage – Torch – Sweety zone

Clem Twitting – Popcorn butter – Drink machine

46. 'It was Lillian Filbert, with the statue of the dog, in the corridor,' said Detective Crapper. 'Well, you did it,' she smiled. 'He said you would. The end-game is near my friend. Will you be brave enough to turn the page?'

Lillian Filbert – Statue of a dog – Corridor

Jill Bisto – Walkie-talkie – Kitchen

Jude Smudge – Bicycle pump – Store room

47. 'It was Poppy Hold, with the tattoo needle, in the waiting room,' said Detective Crapper. Poppy Hold stood up suddenly. 'Get ready, Detective!' she screamed. 'He's going to tattoo his name on your heart! The same letters, again and again!'

Scratch Johnson – Jewelled skull – Design corner

Poppy Hold – Tattoo needle – Waiting area

Josh Williams – Mop – Tattoo chair

48. 'It was John Smith, with the sack of cacao, in the tasting booth,' said Detective Crapper. 'You'll never make it stick,' said John Smith. 'We have the finest lawyers that money can buy. And we control everyone – the press, the politicians, the sweetshops. Our parent company Fray Timor has fingers in every pie.'

Renee Buffet – A knife – Hot chocolate bar

Reg Trembly – Bottle of licquer – Flavour machine

John Smith – Sack of cacao – Tasting booth

49. 'It was Fred Quimby, with the kettle, in the toilet,' said Detective Crapper. Fred smiled. 'I'm an old man, Detective,' he said 'I've lived my life. But to him, we're all like those models.' At that exact moment, Detective Crapper's radio went off. 'Guv, you need to get here now!'

Alabaster Snark – Church spire – City centre

Fred Quimby – Kettle – Toilet

Glen Bishop – Model train – Coast

50. 'It was Arty Froim, with the Thermos flask, in the bar,' said Detective Crapper. At first, Arty Froim looked shocked. Then he started to smile. He clapped, slowly at first, then faster and faster. The lights went out. Then Arty Froim's voice came over the theatre speakers. 'Oh, well done, well done, Detective. You've followed the trail of breadcrumbs and it's led you here. Well, it's me, it's always been me. Arty Froim, Mr Iota Fry, Tom Friary, Mr Ray Foti, Mr Fairtoy. All me. Have you worked it out yet? Morifarty. Pulling the strings. But I wasn't always called Morifarty. I used to be called Daniel Booger. Do you remember, Thomas C?! When you accused me of stealing your potty? YOU RUINED MY LIFE!'

The lights came back on but Arty wasn't on the stage.

Detective Crapper looked up. 'Back to work, lads,' he barked. 'We'll get him next time...'

Also by the author:

War and Poos

Great Constipations

The Lion, The Witch and The Bathroom

A Restroom with a View

David Plopperfield

No s**t,
Sherlock